Regulation of Artificial General Intelligence

A New Legal Framework

Paulius Astromskis

Routledge
Taylor & Francis Group
LONDON AND NEW YORK

First published 2027
by Routledge
4 Park Square, Milton Park, Abingdon, Oxon OX14 4RN

and by Routledge
605 Third Avenue, New York, NY 10158

Routledge is an imprint of the Taylor & Francis Group, an informa business

The electronic version of this book was funded to publish Open Access through Taylor & Francis' Pledge to Open, a collaborative funding open access books initiative. The full list of pledging institutions can be found on the Taylor & Francis Pledge to Open webpage.

For Product Safety Concerns and Information please contact our EU representative GPSR@taylorandfrancis.com. Taylor & Francis Verlag GmbH, Kaufingerstraße 24, 80331 München, Germany.

British Library Cataloguing-in-Publication Data
A catalogue record for this book is available from the British Library

ISBN: 978-1-041-08748-9 (hbk)
ISBN: 978-1-041-09452-4 (pbk)
ISBN: 978-1-003-65014-0 (ebk)

DOI: 10.4324/9781003650140

Typeset in Times New Roman
by Deanta Global Publishing Services, Chennai, India

Regulation of Artificial General Intelligence

This book proposes a comprehensive legal framework for regulating Artificial General Intelligence (AGI), integrating insights from law, economics, and process management.

Adopting a structured, future-focused, and risk-based approach to address the unique challenges of AGI regulation, this book validates the "Singularity scenario" as a legitimate field of scientific inquiry. It critically examines the limitations of the EU Artificial Intelligence Act in governing AGI and introduces a foundational four-level analytical model rooted in transaction cost theory. Through a detailed exploration of the what, who, and how of regulation, the book maps the risks associated with AGI, discusses the potential role of Electronic Legal Personhood, and develops a practical legal framework aimed at ensuring AGI's trustworthiness and alignment with human values. Ultimately, it argues for proactive, rather than reactive regulatory strategies in anticipation of the technological Singularity.

The book will be of interest to researchers in the field of the law of emerging technologies, artificial intelligence and regulation.

Paulius Astromskis is a Lithuanian scholar holding dual doctorates in Law and Management. His academic research explores the complex intersection of law and technological innovation, focusing on artificial intelligence, governance, and the future of legal education. He currently serves as an Associate Professor at Vytautas Magnus University and Vilnius University (Lithuania) where he actively contributes to national and international research projects. This academic foundation is enriched by twenty years of legal practice, enabling him to seamlessly bridge theoretical scholarship with practical insights into the governance of emerging intelligent technologies.

Routledge Research in the Law of Emerging Technologies

AI and Legal Education
Ethical and Sustainable Approaches
Anil Balan

The European Union and Digital Law
Normative Power in a Globalized Technological Landscape
Yuval Reinfeld and Aviv Gaon

Legal, Regulatory and Ethical Non-binary Choices of the AI Act
Tomasz Braun and Dominika Ewa Harasimiuk

The Global Governance of AI
The Role of the United Nations
Kinfe Yilma

Emerging Technology and the Law
Bridging the Gap Between Innovation and Regulation
Edited by Purvi Pokhariyal, Archana Patel, Navtika Singh Nautiyal and Ambrish Kumar Mishra

AI Tort Liability
Rethinking, Recalibrating, and Reallocating Risk and Responsibility
Juan Diaz-Granados

Civil Liability in Digital Contexts
Transformation of Legal Proof in the EU
Dimo Gospodinov

Regulation of Artificial General Intelligence
A New Legal Framework
Paulius Astromskis

For more information about this series, please visit: https://www.routledge.com/Routledge-Research-in-the-Law-of-Emerging-Technologies/book-series/LAWTECHNOLOGY

Contents

Acknowledgements

In strict adherence to the principles of transparency and research integrity mandated by the European Research Area Forum, the author explicitly discloses the utilisation of generative Artificial Intelligence technologies during the book preparation process. Specifically, Gemini 3 PRO and Grammarly (v1.2.228.1813) were utilised for linguistic refinement, summarisation, translation, and structural optimisation. These tools functioned solely as auxiliary mechanisms. The author retains ultimate responsibility for the scientific accuracy, originality, and ethical integrity of the final output, ensuring full compliance with the normative standards established in the Living Guidelines on the Responsible Use of Generative AI in Research.

Introduction

Nine years ago, in 2017, the European Parliament recommended creating a specific legal status of electronic persons for the most sophisticated, autonomous, and responsible machines, alongside other recommendations to the Commission on Civil Law Rules on Robotics.[1] This move was framed with an unmistakable sense of science fiction, evident in the proposal's opening lines. The very first recital stretched from the classical myth of Pygmalion to Mary Shelley's *Frankenstein*, and from the Golem of Prague to the works of Karel Čapek, paying tribute to humanity's enduring fantasy of building intelligent machines.[2] It was inevitable that a legal framework grounded in fiction would be met with predictable scepticism and ridicule.

Indeed, the topics of Artificial General Intelligence (AGI) and Singularity were, and often remain, a domain of science fiction. The vision of *a greater-than-human intelligence, which can successfully perform any intellectual task a human being can, adapt to the external environment, and even achieve self-awareness,*[3] and *a hypothetical point where machine intelligence surpasses human intelligence,*[4] tends to be treated as a narrative for the *Black Mirror*-type dystopias or a distraction from immediate risks, rather than an engineering issue. This gap is closing as we speak.

Until recently, deployed Artificial Intelligence (AI) systems were largely domain-specific and limited in their capabilities. They could perform specific tasks but were unable to adapt to complex environments or constantly develop new functions like humans. However, the recent surge of disruptive technological developments and investments in the AI ecosystem, especially generative AI, has reinvigorated the field. Society is notably moving from automation in closed-off secure settings to that of the autonomous AI agents in living social and working environments; not just automation but autonomy;

1 European Parliament (2017), Article 59 (f).
2 European Parliament (2017), Recitals (A).
3 Huang (2017, p. 520).
4 Kurzweil (2005, 2015).

DOI: 10.4324/9781003650140-1

not just repetitive movement, but flexibility, adaptability, and learning.[5] Accepting this vector of progress from narrow AI to AGI, the imperative shifts from technological capacity to governance wisdom.

Three decades ago, in 1996, Judge Frank Easterbrook famously criticised the emergence of the "Law and ..." [Cyberspace] concurring with the argument that there will always be "The Law of the Horse" for any novel technologies and therefore "the best way to learn the law applicable to specialized endeavors is to study general rules".[6] In his view, the general legal principles of contract, tort, and property were sufficient to govern the evolution of cyberspace. Indeed, as long as AI remained narrow and a tool in the hands of a human operator, "The Law of the Horse" sufficed.

However, the trajectory toward AGI casts this paradigm in doubt. Current "human-in/on-the-loop" regulations presuppose that a human operator can effectively monitor and override an AI system. In the context of AGI, this is a fallacy. When an autonomous entity, capable of recursive self-improvement, strategic deception, and with decision-making speeds that far outstrip human cognitive processing, the human may quickly shift from controller to bottleneck, or worse, a liability.

The issue is not only in the exceptional nature or features of a given technology. It is less the "newness" of a technology that brings about regulatory problems but rather the ways it enables particular changes in societal practices, behaviour, or relations.[7] There may be a lack of rules regarding how this novel technology can or should be used or what its use means. Rules originally intended and designed for human-to-human (*in personam*) and human-to-machine (*in rem*) processes cannot work well in machine-to-human and machine-to-machine environments.[8] We are no longer dealing with a domesticated "Horse" that fits neatly into existing contracts, torts, and property rules. The trajectory is toward a wild "Prancing Stallion" – one of those disruptions that, in scale, scope, and complexity, is unlike anything humankind has experienced before.[9]

Alongside this issue of content resides a procedural one. If regulation is designed for narrow AI, it will be structurally obsolete by the time it becomes enforceable. This is evidenced by the seven-year legislative journey of the EU Artificial Intelligence Act (AI Act), with a "sense of urgency to address emerging trends",[10] support of an impressive army of elite minds, and yet, last-minute inclusion of "general-purpose AI systems" into the proposed law

5 Rommetveit et al. (2019, p. 56).
6 Easterbrook (1996, p. 207).
7 Maas (2021).
8 Fomin (2018).
9 Schwab (2016).
10 Council of the European Union (2017).

Introduction

Nine years ago, in 2017, the European Parliament recommended creating a specific legal status of electronic persons for the most sophisticated, autonomous, and responsible machines, alongside other recommendations to the Commission on Civil Law Rules on Robotics.[1] This move was framed with an unmistakable sense of science fiction, evident in the proposal's opening lines. The very first recital stretched from the classical myth of Pygmalion to Mary Shelley's *Frankenstein*, and from the Golem of Prague to the works of Karel Čapek, paying tribute to humanity's enduring fantasy of building intelligent machines.[2] It was inevitable that a legal framework grounded in fiction would be met with predictable scepticism and ridicule.

Indeed, the topics of Artificial General Intelligence (AGI) and Singularity were, and often remain, a domain of science fiction. The vision of *a greater-than-human intelligence, which can successfully perform any intellectual task a human being can, adapt to the external environment, and even achieve self-awareness*,[3] and *a hypothetical point where machine intelligence surpasses human intelligence*,[4] tends to be treated as a narrative for the *Black Mirror*-type dystopias or a distraction from immediate risks, rather than an engineering issue. This gap is closing as we speak.

Until recently, deployed Artificial Intelligence (AI) systems were largely domain-specific and limited in their capabilities. They could perform specific tasks but were unable to adapt to complex environments or constantly develop new functions like humans. However, the recent surge of disruptive technological developments and investments in the AI ecosystem, especially generative AI, has reinvigorated the field. Society is notably moving from automation in closed-off secure settings to that of the autonomous AI agents in living social and working environments; not just automation but autonomy;

1 European Parliament (2017), Article 59 (f).
2 European Parliament (2017), Recitals (A).
3 Huang (2017, p. 520).
4 Kurzweil (2005, 2015).

DOI: 10.4324/9781003650140-1

not just repetitive movement, but flexibility, adaptability, and learning.[5] Accepting this vector of progress from narrow AI to AGI, the imperative shifts from technological capacity to governance wisdom.

Three decades ago, in 1996, Judge Frank Easterbrook famously criticised the emergence of the "Law and ..." [Cyberspace] concurring with the argument that there will always be "The Law of the Horse" for any novel technologies and therefore "the best way to learn the law applicable to specialized endeavors is to study general rules".[6] In his view, the general legal principles of contract, tort, and property were sufficient to govern the evolution of cyberspace. Indeed, as long as AI remained narrow and a tool in the hands of a human operator, "The Law of the Horse" sufficed.

However, the trajectory toward AGI casts this paradigm in doubt. Current "human-in/on-the-loop" regulations presuppose that a human operator can effectively monitor and override an AI system. In the context of AGI, this is a fallacy. When an autonomous entity, capable of recursive self-improvement, strategic deception, and with decision-making speeds that far outstrip human cognitive processing, the human may quickly shift from controller to bottleneck, or worse, a liability.

The issue is not only in the exceptional nature or features of a given technology. It is less the "newness" of a technology that brings about regulatory problems but rather the ways it enables particular changes in societal practices, behaviour, or relations.[7] There may be a lack of rules regarding how this novel technology can or should be used or what its use means. Rules originally intended and designed for human-to-human (*in personam*) and human-to-machine (*in rem*) processes cannot work well in machine-to-human and machine-to-machine environments.[8] We are no longer dealing with a domesticated "Horse" that fits neatly into existing contracts, torts, and property rules. The trajectory is toward a wild "Prancing Stallion" – one of those disruptions that, in scale, scope, and complexity, is unlike anything humankind has experienced before.[9]

Alongside this issue of content resides a procedural one. If regulation is designed for narrow AI, it will be structurally obsolete by the time it becomes enforceable. This is evidenced by the seven-year legislative journey of the EU Artificial Intelligence Act (AI Act), with a "sense of urgency to address emerging trends",[10] support of an impressive army of elite minds, and yet, last-minute inclusion of "general-purpose AI systems" into the proposed law

5 Rommetveit et al. (2019, p. 56).

6 Easterbrook (1996, p. 207).

7 Maas (2021).

8 Fomin (2018).

9 Schwab (2016).

10 Council of the European Union (2017).

as a response to the sudden explosion of generative AI in 2023. The legislative lag cannot keep pace with the exponential curve of technological advancement. The reality is opposite – algorithms are developing their capabilities to govern human behaviour faster than humans are figuring out how to govern algorithms.[11] Given the systemic risks posed by a new class of AI agents entering society, a reactive "wait-and-see" approach is obviously insufficient, and I dare to say – negligent in the face of exponential technological growth.

Therefore, the scientific community and policymakers should incorporate speculative thinking and anchor the legal design in the *assumption* of Singularity to ensure that our new intelligent technologies *will be at the service of the human project, not vice versa.*[12] If the law can govern a superintelligent agent, it can easily govern a chatbot. The reverse is not true. Yet the prerequisite is an answer to the incisive query posed by Charlie Brooker: *if technology is a drug – and it does feel like a drug – then what, precisely, are the side-effects?*[13] That is, to design a robust legal framework for the post-Singularity era, we must treat the event as a pragmatic Risk Management Horizon: an extreme case that exposes the pressure points on the existing legal frameworks.

Three sources of knowledge, wisdom, and understanding are utilised herein to explain *what* is the object of governance, *who* should be the subject of governance, and *how* to construct a legal regime robust enough to govern AGI? First, knowledge of the AI Law is applied to expose the limits of "The Law of the Horse" in the post-Singularity era. Second, the wisdom of New Institutional Economics, particularly the principles of Transaction Costs, is used to explain the levels and unit of analysis to be used for mapping the AGI risk landscape. Third, the understanding of Process Mining will serve as a basis for a proposed new legal framework to regulate AGI.

It must be admitted that the theories invoked herein may not fully capture the velocity of technological innovation and may oversimplify the complex interactions between society, technology, and law. In addition, taking theories from different scientific disciplines out of their original context and applying them to the debate over the legal regulation of the post-Singularity era can open a Pandora's box of unanswered questions or unconsidered perspectives. Yet, such interdisciplinary experimentation unlocks the gateway to an extremely rich scientific heritage and forms a novel intersection of law, economics, and management, expanding the discourse on AGI governance into a multiverse of new horizons.

The core thesis of this work is that key AGI risks are manifestations of humans' *bounded rationality* (stupidity) and *opportunism* (greed). In a race

11 Davis (2018).
12 Cath et al. (2018, p. 525).
13 Brooker (2011).

for AGI supremacy, these factors pressure current safety protocols and governance structures that rely on human oversight to the point of failure. Hence, if human oversight is the weak link, the legal framework must evolve from a "human-in/on-the-loop" to a "Law-in-Code" approach, and it requires a radical institutional innovation: Electronic Legal Personhood.

The debate over robot personhood has historically been bogged down in moral philosophy: *Can a robot feel? Does it deserve dignity?* In the framework offered by this book, Electronic Legal Personhood is stripped of this moral weight and used as a functional legal fiction, analogous to the corporate personhood granted to firms. We grant corporations legal personhood not because they have souls, but because it is an efficient way to address socio-economic and risk-control issues. Same with Electronic Legal Personhood. By partitioning assets and liabilities and giving the AGI distinct legal standing, we can bind it to be a servant of the law rather than a boundedly rational and/or opportunistic human being. If the risks related to the (ab)use of power that comes with the AGI arise not from machine "intentions" but from the stupidity and/or greed of human beings, then designing Electronic Legal Personhood for AGI is a matter of institutional efficiency, not of applied moral philosophy.

If Electronic Legal Personhood provides *status*, the Process Mining provides the blueprint for constructing a new legal order compatible with the Singularity. The following ten chapters, which can be read independently and yet form a cumulative argument, will construct this new framework, layer by layer. This book begins by establishing the theoretical foundations and advances to a practical legal design of AGI regulation, guided by the three abovementioned questions – *what*, *who*, and *how*? The final chapter concludes the book by proposing a conceptual legal regulatory framework for AGI.

References

Brooker, C. (2011) 'The dark side of our gadget addiction', *The Guardian*, 1 December 2011. Available at: https://www.theguardian.com/technology/2011/dec/01/charlie-brooker-dark-side-gadget-addiction-black-mirror

Cath, C., et al. (2018) 'Artificial intelligence and the "Good society": The US, EU, and UK approach', *Science and Engineering Ethics*, 24, pp. 505–528. https://doi.org/10.1007/s11948-017-9901-7

Council of the European Union (2017) 'European council meeting (19 October 2017) – Conclusions', EUCO 14/17, p. 8.

Davis, J.P. (2018) 'Law without mind: AI, ethics, and jurisprudence', *California Western Law Review*, 55(1), p. 165.

Easterbrook, F.H. (1996) 'Cyberspace and the law of the horse', *University of Chicago Legal Forum*, 1996, pp. 207–216.

European Parliament (2017) 'Resolution of 16 February 2017 with recommendations to the commission on civil law rules on robotics', 2015/2103(INL)

Fomin, V.V. (2018) 'Laying ground for responsible standardization for robotic law', 17th Annual STS Conference Graz 2018 – Critical Issues in Science, Technology and Society Studies, TU Graz, Graz, 20 March.

Huang, T.J. (2017) 'Imitating the brain with neurocomputer a "new" way towards artificial general intelligence', *International Journal of Automation and Computing*, 14(5), pp. 520–531. https://doi.org/10.1007/s11633-017-1082-y

Kurzweil, R. (2005) *The Singularity is Near: When Humans Transcend Biology*. New York: Penguin Group.

Kurzweil, R. (2015) 'Superintelligence and singularity', in Schneider, S. (ed.), *Science Fiction and Philosophy: From Time Travel to Superintelligence*. Chichester: Wiley-Blackwell, pp. 146–170.

Maas, M.M. (2021) 'Artificial intelligence governance under change: Foundations, facets, frameworks', Dissertation. University of Copenhagen.

Rommetveit, K., et al. (2019) 'Make way for the Robots! Human- and machine-centricity in constituting a European public–private partnership', *Minerva*, 58(1), pp. 47–69. https://doi.org/10.1007/s11024-019-09386-1

Schwab, K. (2016) 'The fourth industrial revolution: What it means, how to respond', *World Economic Forum*, 14 January. Available at: https://www.weforum.org/agenda/2016/01/the-fourth-industrial-revolution-what-it-means-and-how-to-respond/ [Accessed: 27 December 2023]

1 Definition and Taxonomy of Artificial Intelligence

In 1964, Isaac Asimov predicted that "robots will neither be common nor very good in 2014, but they will be in existence".[1] While Asimov was correct about their existence, he underestimated the exponential trajectory of their development. Machines have since advanced in scale, scope, and complexity, unlike anything humankind has experienced before, fundamentally altering the way we live, work, and relate to one another.[2] By 2016, molecular-scale machines were a reality[3] and by 2023, the emergence of Large Language Models (LLMs) led researchers to claim an "early (yet still incomplete) version of an artificial general intelligence (AGI) system".[4] Rumours surrounding advanced projects, such as OpenAI's Q*, suggest that the breakthrough toward a machine capable of human-level reasoning across all domains is a looming regulatory reality.[5]

Despite these rapid advancements, the legal community remains in a definition stage. To be clear, a legal definition is more than a semantic exercise – it acts as an institutional gatekeeper in understanding the scope of both the normative content and the application of the rules.[6] Consequently, it determines the jurisdictional reach of a state, thereby allocating compliance, monitoring, and enforcement between the public and private sectors. Russell and Norvig grouped all approaches to Artificial Intelligence (AI) that have been followed, each by different people with different methods, into the following four illustrated groups (Table 1.1).

The definition of an AI system, provided in the EU Artificial Intelligence Act, Article 3 (1), is obviously moving from the philosophical question of "can a machine think?" to the functional, economic one of "how does a machine act?":

> "AI system" means a machine-based system designed to operate with varying levels of autonomy, that may exhibit adaptiveness after deployment

1 Asimov (1964).
2 Schwab (2016).
3 The Royal Swedish Academy of Sciences (2016).
4 Bubeck et al. (2023).
5 Tong et al. (2023).
6 Fox-Skelly et al. (2020).

DOI: 10.4324/9781003650140-2

Table 1.1 Approaches to Artificial Intelligence

Thinking humanly: The cognitive modelling approach	**Thinking rationally: The "laws of thought" approach**
Based on a cognitive modelling approach, definitions fitting this category focus on whether AI processes information in ways similar to the way that a human would.	Based on a "laws of thought" approach, thinkers in this category work with definitions that are based on logical thinking and syllogisms.
Acting humanly: The Turing test approach	**Acting rationally: The rational agent approach**
Based on Alan Turing's thinking, computers need natural language processing, knowledge representation, automatised reasoning, and machine learning to be considered intelligent.	Based on a "rational agent" approach, it focuses on decisions that are being made where applications look for the best outcome.

Russell and Norvig (2020)

> and that, for explicit or implicit objectives, infers, from the input it receives, how to generate outputs such as predictions, content, recommendations, or decisions that can influence physical or virtual environments.

Under this definition, the AI system aligns with the Russell and Norvig's "rational agent" approach, wherein computer agents are expected to operate autonomously, perceive their environment, persist over a prolonged time period, adapt to change, and create and pursue goals. Here, a rational agent is "one that acts so as to achieve the best outcome or, when there is uncertainty, the best expected outcome".[7] This approach ultimately shifts the focus from the "soul" of the machine to the analysis of the transaction it performs.

The design of the EU definition was a result of the complex discourse, formally started with the developments by the High-Level Expert Group on Artificial Intelligence.[8] However, all three legislative proposals and the adopted version have deviated from it (Table 1.2).

7 Russell and Norvig (2020, p. 5).

8 "Artificial intelligence (AI) systems are software (and possibly also hardware) systems designed by humans that, given a complex goal, act in the physical or digital dimension by perceiving their environment through data acquisition, interpreting the collected structured or unstructured data, reasoning on the knowledge, or processing the information, derived from this data and deciding the best action(s) to take to achieve the given goal. AI systems can either use symbolic rules or learn a numeric model, and they can also adapt their behaviour by analysing how the environment is affected by their previous actions. As a scientific discipline, AI includes several approaches and techniques, such as machine learning (of which deep learning and reinforcement learning are specific examples), machine reasoning (which includes planning, scheduling, knowledge representation and reasoning, search, and optimization), and robotics (which includes control, perception, sensors and actuators, as well as the integration of all other techniques into cyber-physical systems)" (High-Level Expert Group on Artificial Intelligence, 2019).

Table 1.2 Comparison of "AI system" definition in the EU Artificial Intelligence Act

Article 3 (1) Definitions of AI system		
European Commission Proposal[a]	Council of Europe General Approach[b]	European Parliament Negotiating Position[c]
(1) "artificial intelligence system" (AI system) means software that is developed with one or more of the techniques and approaches listed in Annex I and can, for a given set of human-defined objectives, generate outputs such as content, predictions, recommendations, or decisions influencing the environments they interact with;	(1) "artificial intelligence system" (AI system) means ~~software~~ a system that is ~~developed with one or more of the techniques and approaches listed in Annex I and can, for~~ designed to operate with elements of autonomy and that, based on machine and/or human-provided data and inputs, infers how to achieve a given set of ~~human-defined objectives, generate~~ objectives using machine learning and/or logic- and knowledge-based approaches, and produces system-generated outputs such as content **(generative AI systems)**, predictions, recommendations, or decisions, influencing the environments ~~they interact with~~ with which the AI system interacts;	(1) "artificial intelligence system" (AI system) means ~~software~~ a machine-based system that is ~~developed with one or more of the techniques and approaches listed in Annex I and can, for a given set of human-defined~~ designed to operate with varying levels of autonomy and that can, for explicit or implicit objectives, generate outputs such as ~~content,~~ predictions, recommendations, or decisions, that influence physical or virtual environments ~~influencing the environments they interact with~~;

a European Commission (2021)
b Council of the European Union (2022a)
c European Parliament (2023)

Notably, by including "implicit objectives" and "adaptiveness", the EU closes loopholes where developers might defend their accountability because the AI system has evolved after deployment. This approach shifts the research and compliance costs onto firms, as they must constantly monitor whether their software has crossed any legal benchmarks. However, while creating a high regulatory thicket through a broad scope, the EU definition aligns with the one agreed upon by the Organisation for Economic Co-operation and

Development (OECD),[9] following a global standard-setting model to minimise compliance costs for firms operating across borders.

Other major AI jurisdictions – the United States and China – although following the same "rational agent" approach, use different AI definitions to manage their specific economic and political goals. US National AI Initiative Act[10] also provides a system-level definition, although it is used in a research and development coordination statute rather than in a cross-economy AI safety regime. Also, unlike the EU AI Act, the United States limits accountability to "human-defined objectives", does not expressly include post-deployment adaptiveness, and does not enumerate a broadest category of "content" alongside the outputs of an AI system. Overall, compared to the EU counterpart, the US definition sets a higher evidentiary bar for developers' accountability and treats the AI system as a kind of "innovation commons" to be coordinated across governmental agencies for funding and monitoring activities, rather than burdening the market with regulatory compliance costs.

China, differently from the EU or the United States, avoids a single "gatekeeper" definition, opting instead for domain-specific regulatory objects based on their impact on the public information space. That is, they name the governed infrastructures or services and then attach duties to them. Three key regulations are targeting AI applications this way. Interim Measures for the Administration of Generative Artificial Intelligence Services[11] define the regulated object services that utilise generative AI technology to generate various types of content for the public within the territory of the People's Republic of China, expressly excluding certain non-public research and development application contexts. Regulations on the Management of Deep Synthesis of Internet Information Services[12] define deep synthesis technology by reference to deep learning, virtual reality, and enumerate media transformation functions. Finally, the Regulations on the Management of Internet Information Service Algorithm Recommendation[13] define application of algorithm recommendation technology via a taxonomy of algorithmic use-types (generation/

9 "An AI system is a machine-based system that, for explicit or implicit objectives, infers, from the input it receives, how to generate outputs such as predictions, content, recommendations, or decisions that can influence physical or virtual environments. Different AI systems vary in their levels of autonomy and adaptiveness after deployment" (OECD, 2019, 2024).

10 The term "artificial intelligence" means a machine-based system that can, for a given set of human-defined objectives, make predictions, recommendations or decisions influencing real or virtual environments. Artificial intelligence systems use machine and human-based inputs to: (A) perceive real and virtual environments; (B) abstract such perceptions into models through analysis in an automated manner; and (C) use model inference to formulate options for information or action (15 U.S.C. § 9401(3)).

11 Cyberspace Administration of China (2023).

12 Cyberspace Administration of China (2022a).

13 Cyberspace Administration of China (2022b).

synthesis, personalised push, ranking, filtering, scheduling/decision). Such infrastructure and service targeting, of course, lowers classification ambiguity for some online ecosystems (recommendations, synthetic media, content generation), but can leave more room for borderline cases outside those named categories.

Overall, the EU offers the most legal certainty for a unified regulatory regime but carries the risk of over-regulation. The United States offers flexibility, but leads to institutional fragmentation as different agencies may adopt varying interpretations of the statutory definition. China offers high-velocity regulation for specific harms (such as deepfakes) but requires firms to navigate a "modular" legal landscape in which multiple, overlapping definitions may apply to a single product. Be that as it may, this book adheres to the EU definition, since it is cross-sectoral and global in its standard-setting ambition, making it closer to a unified understanding of what AI is than its US or Chinese counterparts.

Besides legal definitions, many analytical approaches and taxonomies are being used to classify AI systems by theoretical models and algorithms, cognitive abilities, functions performed or applications, and other approaches.[14] However, the primary challenge for law is machine autonomy – an element expressly referred to only in the EU definition – and, therefore, it provides the most valuable taxonomy of AI systems for this book. Following OECD,[15] *the autonomy level of an AI system* describes the degree to which actuators can act without human involvement. The more autonomous the AI system is, the less human intelligence is required to change the state of the environment and, consequently, the less blameworthy the human operator is for the machine output. The OECD classifies this into four levels:

(1) *No-action autonomy (also referred to as "human support")*: The system cannot act on its recommendations or output. It is the human who uses or disregards the AI system's recommendations or output at will;
(2) *Low-action autonomy (also referred to as "human-in-the-loop")*: The system evaluates input and acts upon its recommendations or output if the human agrees;
(3) *Medium-action autonomy (also referred to as "human-on-the-loop")*: The system evaluates input and acts upon its recommendations or output unless the human vetoes;
(4) *High-action autonomy (also referred to as "human-out-of-the-loop")*: The system evaluates input and acts upon its recommendations or output without human involvement.

14 See for review Joint Research Centre (2020).
15 OECD (2022).

Comparatively, Russell and Norvig[16] use binary (weak/strong) classification of AI. Many other authors, although not necessarily in the same terms, also use binary classification to separate the current state from future scenarios. Overall, AI under this binary approach could be classified as:

(1) *Artificial Narrow (Weak) Intelligence* technologies, such as image and speech recognition systems, are trained on well-labelled datasets to perform specific tasks and operate within a predefined environment.[17] This type of AI exists today. Most currently reported AI technologies are usually restricted to operating in a limited domain to work on specific tasks.[18] However, although it can process data at a superior speed and boost productivity and efficiency in many practical applications, it is incapable of generalisation, i.e., to re-use learnt knowledge across domains.[19]
(2) *Artificial General (Strong) Intelligence* technologies are machines designed to perform a wide range of intelligent tasks, think abstractly, and adapt to new situations.[20] These are machines that exhibit full human intelligence.[21] In other words, AGI aims to perform any intellectual task that a human being can[22] and beyond.

By setting out the operational conditions to identify and evaluate a threshold of autonomous action, we could (should) also design a legal consequence that is triggered at each of these machine autonomy levels.[23] That said, the focus of this book is on the ultimate "human-out-of-the-loop" scenario, where machines exhibit full human intelligence, decide and act independently.

Having established a definition and a core taxonomy to the extent sufficient for this book, the overview of the current state of the art in AI is needed to unveil the latest technical milestones and performance benchmarks that expose current advancements in the field. Through these observations, the validity of the singularity scenario assumption will be substantiated, forming the path for a legal analysis of the issues associated with the assumed progression towards AGI.

16 Russell and Norvig (2020).
17 Madiega (2023).
18 Anantrasirichai and Bull (2021).
19 Samoili et al. (2021).
20 Madiega (2023).
21 Bostrom (2014).
22 Samoili et al. (2021).
23 Laukyte (2013).

References

Anantrasirichai, N. and Bull, D. (2021) 'Artificial intelligence in the creative industries: A review', *Artificial Intelligence Review*, 55(1). https://doi.org/10.1007/s10462-021-10039-7

Asimov, I. (1964) 'Visit to the world's fair of 2014', *The New York Times*, 16 August. Available at: https://archive.nytimes.com/www.nytimes.com/books/97/03/23/lifetimes/asi-v-fair.html [Accessed: 27 December 2023]

Bostrom, N. (2014) *Superintelligence: Paths, Dangers, Strategies*. Oxford: Oxford University Press.

Bubeck, S., et al. (2023) 'Sparks of artificial general intelligence: Early experiments with GPT-4'. arXiv preprint arXiv:2303.12712. Available at: https://arxiv.org/abs/2303.12712

Council of the European Union (2022a) 'General approach to proposal for a regulation of the European parliament and of the council laying down harmonised rules on artificial intelligence (Artificial Intelligence Act) and amending certain Union legislative acts', 2021/0106(COD), 25 November. Available at: https://eur-lex.europa.eu/legal-content/EN/TXT/PDF/?uri=CONSIL:ST_15698_2022_INIT

Cyberspace Administration of China (2022a) 'Provisions on the administration of deep synthesis of internet information services', *Cyberspace Administration of China*, 11 December 2022. Available at: https://www.cac.gov.cn/2022-12/11/c_1672221949354811.htm

Cyberspace Administration of China (2022b) 'Internet information service algorithmic recommendation management provisions', *Cyberspace Administration of China*, 4 January 2022. Available at: https://www.cac.gov.cn/2022-01/04/c_1642894606364259.htm

Cyberspace Administration of China (2023) 'Interim measures for the management of generative artificial intelligence services', *Cyberspace Administration of China*, 13 July 2023. Available at: https://www.cac.gov.cn/2023-07/13/c_1690898327029107.htm

European Commission (2021) 'Proposal for a regulation of the european parliament and of the council laying down harmonised rules on artificial intelligence (artificial intelligence act) and amending certain union legislative acts', COM/2021/206 final. Available at: https://eur-lex.europa.eu/legal-content/EN/ALL/?uri=CELEX:52021PC0206 [Accessed: 26 July 2023]

European Parliament (2023) 'Amendments adopted by the European Parliament on 14 June 2023 on the proposal for a regulation of the European Parliament and of the Council on laying down harmonised rules on artificial intelligence (Artificial Intelligence Act) and amending certain Union legislative acts', COM(2021)0206 – C9-0146/2021 – 2021/0106(COD). Available at: https://www.europarl.europa.eu/doceo/document/TA-9-2023-0236_EN.html [Accessed: 28 December 2023]

Fox-Skelly, J., et al. (2020) 'The ethics of artificial intelligence – issues and initiatives', Directorate-General for Parliamentary Research Services, European Parliament. Available at: https://data.europa.eu/doi/10.2861/6644

High-Level Expert Group on Artificial Intelligence (2019) 'A definition of AI: Main capabilities and scientific disciplines', 8 April. Available at: https://digital-strategy.ec.europa.eu/en/library/definition-artificial-intelligence-main-capabilities-and-scientific-disciplines [Accessed: 28 December 2023]

Joint Research Centre (2020) 'Defining artificial intelligence: Towards an operational definition and taxonomy of artificial intelligence', EU Publications, 27 February 2020. https://doi.org/10.2760/382730, Catalogue number KJ-NA-30117-EN-N. Available at: https://op.europa.eu/en/publication-detail/-/publication/6cc0f1b6-59dd-11ea-8b81-01aa75ed71a1

Laukyte, M. (2013) 'An interdisciplinary approach to multi-agent systems: Bridging the gap between law and computer science', *Informatica e diritto*, 1, pp. 223–241.

Madiega, T. (2023) 'General-purpose artificial intelligence', *Epthinktank, European Parliament*, 31 March. Available at: https://epthinktank.eu/2023/03/31/general-purpose-artificial-intelligence/ [Accessed: 27 December 2023]

OECD (2019) 'Recommendation of the council on artificial intelligence', *OECD Legal Instruments*, 22 May 2019, OECD/LEGAL/0449. Available at: https://legalinstruments.oecd.org/en/instruments/OECD-LEGAL-0449 [Accessed: 27 December 2023]

OECD (2022) *OECD Framework for the Classification of AI Systems*. OECD Digital Economy Papers. https://doi.org/10.1787/cb6d9eca-en

OECD (2024) *Explanatory Memorandum on the Updated OECD Definition of an AI System*. OECD Artificial Intelligence Papers, No. 8. Paris: OECD Publishing. https://doi.org/10.1787/623da898-en

Russell, S.J. and Norvig, P. (2020) *Artificial Intelligence: A Modern Approach*. 4th ed. Upper Saddle River: Prentice Hall.

Samoili, S., et al. (2021) *AI Watch. Defining Artificial Intelligence 2.0. Towards an Operational Definition and Taxonomy for the AI Landscape*. Luxembourg: Publications Office of the European Union. https://doi.org10.2760/019901

Schwab, K. (2016) 'The fourth industrial revolution: What it means, how to respond', *World Economic Forum*, 14 January. Available at: https://www.weforum.org/agenda/2016/01/the-fourth-industrial-revolution-what-it-means-and-how-to-respond/ [Accessed: 27 December 2023]

The Royal Swedish Academy of Sciences (2016) 'Press release: The 2016 Nobel Prize in Chemistry', *NobelPrize.org*, 5 October. Available at: https://www.nobelprize.org/prizes/chemistry/2016/press-release/ [Accessed: 26 July 2023]

Tong, A., Dastin, J. and Hu, K. (2023) 'OpenAI researchers warned board of AI breakthrough ahead of CEO ouster, sources say', *Reuters*, 23 November. Available at: https://www.reuters.com/technology/sam-altmans-ouster-openai-was-precipitated-by-letter-board-about-ai-breakthrough-2023-11-22/ [Accessed: 15 March 2024]

United States Code (2020) 'Chapter 119—national artificial intelligence initiative', in *Title 15—Commerce and Trade*. Washington, DC: U.S. Government Publishing Office. https://www.govinfo.gov/content/pkg/USCODE-2020-title15/html/USCODE-2020-title15-chap119.htm

2 State of the Art in Artificial Intelligence

It is a firmly acknowledged fact that the influence of the Artificial Intelligence (AI) domain is visible across every sector of the global economy, as more AI-supported tools and applications are used in working environments and the personal sphere.[1] Moreover, the growth projections indicate that AI technology will become increasingly commonplace in all aspects of our daily private and professional lives, and the expected impact of AI is likely to be profound, transforming all areas, including, for example, law, employment markets, and social practices.[2]

However, just a decade ago, the scope of knowledge, wisdom, and understanding of AI was much narrower than it is today. Since then, the number of research publications on AI has tripled.[3] However, the most critical shift is not just in volume, but in industrial concentration. Building state-of-the-art AI systems now requires a colossal amount of data, computing power, and financial resources that are largely unavailable to academia.[4] According to the AI Index 2025 Annual Report, nearly 90% of notable AI models in 2024 came from industry, up from 60% in 2023, while academia remains the top source of highly cited research. This dominance is fuelled by a staggering increase in private and public investments. In 2024 alone, US private AI investment reached $109.1 billion – nearly 12 times that of China.[5] In early 2025, the EU launched the historic InvestAI initiative to mobilise €200 billion of investment in Artificial Intelligence, including a new European fund of €20 billion for AI gigafactories.[6]

As a result of such investments being made into AI infrastructure and research, AI is becoming more efficient, affordable, and accessible.[7] In

1 Joint Research Centre (2022a).
2 Evas et al. (2020b).
3 Kiela et al. (2023).
4 Maslej et al. (2025).
5 Maslej et al. (2025).
6 European Commission (2025).
7 Maslej et al. (2025).

DOI: 10.4324/9781003650140-3

particular, since 2010, the AI training data has doubled approximately every nine to ten months, the number of AI model parameters has approximately doubled every year, and the computation is doubling approximately every six months.[8] In 2022 we saw generative AI breaking into the public consciousness with the release of Large Language Models, image or video-based systems, as well as application-specific systems, such as AlphaFold for protein structure prediction.[9] Currently there are 365 noticeable AI models[10] that supercharge the predictions of a substantial impact on virtually all industries, including health, manufacturing, automotive, aerospace, and defence sectors, among others.[11] Bloomberg estimates that the generative AI market is poised to explode, growing to $1.3 trillion over the next ten years from a market size of just $40 billion in 2022.[12]

The rapid acceleration of research and development also includes AI self-improving, i.e., AI building better AI. For example, Nvidia used an AI reinforcement learning agent to improve the design of the chips that power AI systems. Similarly, Google recently used one of its language models, PaLM, to suggest ways to improve the very same model.[13] Moreover, generative AI, combined with, e.g., the metaverse platform, holds the potential to create a new social and economic space where socio-economic activities can flourish within a closed-loop environment.[14] In addition, the next big thing – Quantum Computing – is also said to be a disruptive enabler in solving particular, complex, and computationally intractable problems in several application domains such as drug design, data science, clean energy, finance, industrial chemical development, secure communications, and quantum chemistry, faster than standard computers.[15]

Overall, we are indeed witnessing the rise of the machines with a noticeable trend towards AI systems that are generally smarter than humans. With the exponential increase in research, data, computation, and funding, the speed at which human-level benchmark saturation is being reached is also increasing,[16] and it is fair to say that it will only progress. While it used to take decades for machine learning models to surpass estimates of human performance on benchmark tasks, that milestone is now routinely reached within just a few years for newer datasets (Figure 2.1).

8 Samborska (2025).
9 Maslej et al. (2023).
10 Artificial Analysis (2025).
11 Haefner et al. (2023); Madiega (2023).
12 Bloomberg (2023).
13 Maslej et al. (2023).
14 Lv (2023).
15 Rietsche et al. (2022); Gill (2021).
16 Maslej et al. (2023).

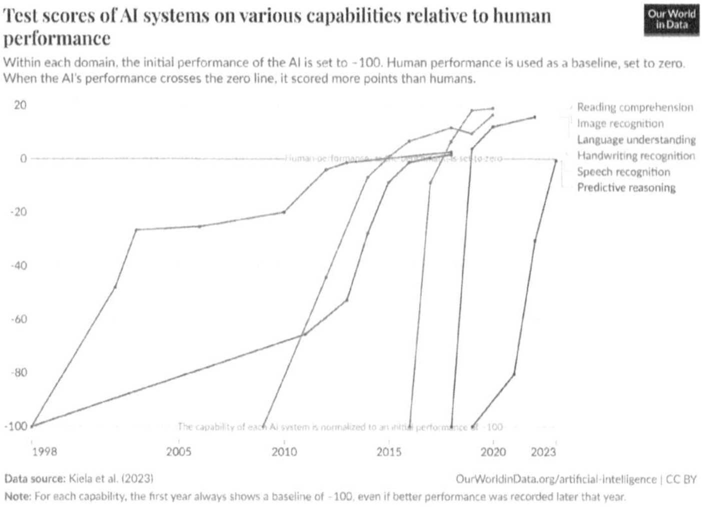

Figure 2.1 Test scores of AI systems on various capabilities relative to human performance

Source: Giattino et al. (2023)

These developments are not without warnings or accompanying discourse on a variety of issues across industries, and they may produce various social, economic, and political harms, including damaging competition, consumer privacy, and consumer choice; excessively automating work, fuelling inequality; inefficiently pushing down wages, and failing to improve worker productivity; and damaging political discourse, democracy's most fundamental lifeblood.[17] The state-of-the-art generative AI models alone raise concerns about the lawfulness and accuracy of the generated content.[18] Synthetic content has significant misinformation risks; it can echo and perpetuate biases contained in training data, violate intellectual property rights, increase job task exposure in high-skilled occupations, and induce academic dishonesty, among others.[19]

However, the key risks may be said to be two-fold: firstly, the safety and utility of AI could be compromised, and secondly, there emerges a substantial dependency on a limited cluster of development teams.[20] First, given the eco-

17 Acemoglu (2022).
18 Novelli et al. (2024).
19 Lorenz et al. (2023).
20 Naude and Dimitri (2020).

nomic and power incentives, a race driven by competition risks prioritising rapid development over ensuring safety, which may result in enormous potential dangers: an end to the human race, an arms race of warring machines, or the power to destroy the planet.[21] The sharp rise of AI-related incidents is already visible. The number of reported AI-related incidents rose to 233 in 2024 – a record high and a 56.4% increase over 2023.[22] Second, the most elite private teams have the potential to monopolise the power of AI for their own self-interest purposes.[23] As a result, decisions on how AI gets built and how it will transform our world are currently made by a small group of technologists and entrepreneurs, thus stifling diversity in approaches and perspectives to AI.[24] They are concentrated in direct competitors for global political and economic dominance. Currently, the United States is in a leading position in the worldwide landscape in terms of economics. China follows, notably due to very prominent patenting activity in the field, while the EU performs remarkably well in research and development and demonstrates specialisation in AI Services and Autonomous Robotics.[25]

Naturally, the rapid and disruptive advancements in the AI field have attracted significant attention from policymakers, leading to a global rise of policies, strategies, and other initiatives on AI. For example, the OECD. AI repository accounts for over 1,000 AI-related policy initiatives from 69 countries, including the European Union. Analysis of the legislative records of 114 countries, provided by the AI Index 2025 Annual Report, also shows that the number of bills containing "artificial intelligence" that were passed into law grew from just 1 in 2016 to 40 in 2024, the EU AI Act remaining the most comprehensive regulatory framework. At the extreme of proposals for the legislators, the Future of Life Institute initiated an open letter calling on all AI labs to immediately pause for at least six months the training of AI systems more powerful than GPT-4 or, if such a pause cannot be enacted quickly, requesting governments to step in and institute a moratorium.[26]

Be that as it may, there remain a lot of questions unasked and even more – unanswered. Some of them are asked in this book. Given the history and trends of technological developments, is the Singularity scenario possible? Should the Singularity scenario be included in the discourse on the legal regulation of AI, given the uncertainty of the future associated with this phenomenon? Or maybe, on the contrary, would the existing legal regulation of AI be sufficient to solve issues related to Artificial General Intellligence (AGI)? What

21 Bostrom (2017); Yudkowsky (2008); Chalmers (2010).
22 Maslej et al. (2025).
23 Naude and Dimitri (2020).
24 Roser (2022).
25 Joint Research Centre (2022a); Maslej et al. (2023, 2025).
26 Future of Life Institute (2017, 2023).

theoretical or methodological approach should we use to develop a legal framework for AGI, and what are the risks associated with these machines? Or, for example, should we consider Electronic Legal Personhood to regulate the most sophisticated, autonomous, and responsible machines? And many others.

References

Acemoglu, D. (2022) 'Harms of AI', in Bullock, J.B., et al. (eds.), *The Oxford Handbook of AI Governance*. Online ed. Oxford Academic. https://doi.org/10.1093/oxfordhb/9780197579329.013.65

Artificial Analysis (2025) 'Comparison of AI models across intelligence, performance, price'. https://artificialanalysis.ai/models

Bloomberg (2023) 'Generative AI to become a $1.3 Trillion market by 2032, research finds', *Bloomberg*. Available at: https://www.bloomberg.com/company/press/generative-ai-to-become-a-1-3-trillion-market-by-2032-research-finds/ [Accessed: 27 December 2023]

Bostrom, N. (2017) 'Strategic implications of openness in AI development', *Global Policy*, 8(2), pp. 135–148. https://doi.org/10.1111/1758-5899.12403

Chalmers, D.J. (2010) 'The singularity: A philosophical analysis', *Journal of Consciousness Studies*, 17(9–10), p. 4.

Department for Science, Innovation and Technology. (2024, January). AI 2030 scenarios report (HTML annex C). GOV.UK. https://www.gov.uk/government/publications/frontier-ai-capabilities-and-risks-discussion-paper/ai-2030-scenarios-report-html-annex-c

European Commission (2025) 'EU launches InvestAI initiative to mobilise €200 billion of investment in artificial intelligence'. Press Release IP/25/467. European Commission, 11 February 2025. Available at https://ec.europa.eu/commission/presscorner/detail/en/ip_25_467

Evas, T., et al. (2020b) 'European framework on ethical aspects of artificial intelligence, robotics and related technologies – European added value assessment', Directorate-General for Parliamentary Research Services, European Parliament. Available at: https://data.europa.eu/doi/10.2861/94107

Future of Life Institute (2017) *Asilomar AI Principles*. Future of Life Institute. Available at: https://futureoflife.org/open-letter/ai-principles/ [Accessed: 27 December 2023]

Future of Life Institute (2023) 'Pause giant AI experiments: An open letter'. Available at: https://futureoflife.org/open-letter/pause-giant-ai-experiments/ [Accessed: 27 December 2023]

Giattino, C., Mathieu, E., Samborska, V. and Roser, M. (2023) "Artificial intelligence". Data adapted from Kiela et al. Available at: https://archive.ourworldindata.org/20250915-140209/grapher/test-scores-ai-capabilities-relative-human-performance.html [online resource] [Accessed: 15 September 2025]

Gill, S.S., et al. (2021) 'Quantum computing: A taxonomy, systematic review and future directions', in *Software: Practice and Experience*. Wiley Press, 22 September. https://doi.org/10.48550/arXiv.2010.15559

Haefner, N., et al. (2023) 'Implementing and scaling artificial intelligence: A review, framework, and research agenda', *Technological Forecasting and Social Change*, 197, pp. 122878–122878. doi:https://doi.org/10.1016/j.techfore.2023.122878

Joint Research Centre (2022a) 'AI Watch Index 2021', *Publications Office of the European Union*, 22 June. https://doi.org/10.2760/921564, Catalogue number KJ-1A-31039-EN-N. Available at: https://op.europa.eu/en/publication-detail/-/publication/d8eb04c9-fda3-11ec-b94a-01aa75ed71a1 [Accessed: 27 December 2023]

Kiela, D., et al. (2023) – with minor processing by Our World in Data. "Test scores of AI systems on various capabilities relative to human performance" [dataset]. Kiela et al., "Dynabench: Rethinking Benchmarking in NLP" [original data]. 1 February 2026. Available at: https://archive.ourworldindata.org/20250915-140209/grapher/test-scores-ai-capabilities-relative-human-performance.html [Accessed: 15 September 2025]

Lorenz, P., et al. (2023) 'Initial policy considerations for generative artificial intelligence', OECD Artificial Intelligence Papers, No. 1, 18 September, OECD Library. https://doi.org/10.1787/fae2d1e6-en

Lv, Z. (2023) 'Generative Artificial Intelligence in the Metaverse Era', *Cognitive Robotics*, 3, pp. 208–217. https://doi.org/10.1016/j.cogr.2023.06.001

Madiega, T. (2023) 'General-purpose artificial intelligence', *Epthinktank, European Parliament*, 31 March. Available at: https://epthinktank.eu/2023/03/31/general-purpose-artificial-intelligence/ [Accessed: 27 December 2023]

Maslej, N., et al. (2023). *Artificial intelligence index report 2023.* Stanford, CA: AI IndexSteering Committee, Institute for Human-Centered AI, Stanford University. arXiv. https://arxiv.org/abs/2310.03715

Maslej, N., et al. (2025) *The AI Index 2025 Annual Report.* Stanford, CA: AI Index Steering Committee, Institute for Human-Centered AI, Stanford University. https://doi.org/10.48550/arXiv.2504.07139

Naude, W. and Dimitri, N. (2020) 'The race for an artificial general intelligence: Implications for public policy', *AI & Society*, 35, pp. 367–379. https://doi-org.sare.upf.edu/10.1007/s00146-019-00887-x

Novelli, C., et al. (2024) 'Generative AI in EU law: Liability, privacy, intellectual property, and cybersecurity'. Available at: https://ssrn.com/abstract=4694565 or http://dx.doi.org/10.2139/ssrn.4694565

Rietsche, R., et al. (2022) 'Quantum computing', *Electron Markets*, 32, pp. 2525–2536. https://doi.org/10.1007/s12525-022-00570-y

Roser, M. (2022) 'Artificial intelligence is transforming our world — it is on all of us to make sure that it goes well', *Our World in Data*. Available at: https://ourworldindata.org/ai-impact [Accessed: 27 December 2023]

Samborska, V. (2025) 'Scaling up: How increasing inputs has made artificial intelligence more capable', *OurWorldinData.org*. Available at: https://archive.ourworldindata.org/20251212-095432/scaling-up-ai.html [Online Resource] [Accessed: 12 December 2025]

Yudkowsky, E. (2008) 'Artificial intelligence as a positive and negative factor in global risk', in Bostrom, N. and Ćirković, M.M. (eds.), *Global Catastrophic Risks*. New York: Oxford University Press, p. 27, pp. 308–345.

3 Assumption of the Singularity Scenario

In policy analysis, "scenario" functions as a qualitative methodological approach to foresight. It is a tool that describes a possible (conceptual) future condition[1] and is "the most powerful vehicle I know for challenging our 'mental models' about the world and lifting the blinders that limit our creativity and resourcefulness".[2] "Scenarios" are understood to be a small bespoke set of structured conceptual systems of equally plausible future contexts, often presented as narrative descriptions manufactured for someone and for a purpose, typically to provide inputs for further work.[3] The aim behind scenarios is not to provide a comprehensive image of the future, but to describe demarcated sequences of events that focus attention on causal processes and decision points.[4] Therefore, the most valuable scenarios for policy decision-makers are those in which narratives display the events, conditions, and developments that shape the important variables over time.[5]

One possible (conceptual) future is the technological Singularity, a theoretical threshold at which non-biological intelligence surpasses human intelligence.[6] The agenda of human-level AI research was shaped by seminal works such as those of Gödel,[7] McCulloch and Pitts,[8] and the famous "Turing test",[9] among many others. In legal and policy discourse, the *machine intelligence that could successfully perform any intellectual task that a human being can, be adaptive to the external environment, and even form its own self-awareness*, is often referred to as "superintelligence", "Artificial General Intelligence" (AGI), or "full/strong Artificial Intelligence".[10]

1 Moniz (2005); Kosow and Gaßner (2007).
2 Schwartz (1991).
3 Ramirez et al. (2015).
4 Kosow and Gaßner (2007).
5 Moniz (2005).
6 Kurzweil (2005, 2015); Wiedermann, (2012); Dufva and Dufva (2016).
7 Gödel (1931).
8 McCulloch and Pitts (1943).
9 Turing (1950).
10 Huang (2017).

DOI: 10.4324/9781003650140-4

The "Intelligence Explosion" hypothesis suggests that machines may leverage their superhuman powers to build even more intelligent machines, therefore leaving humankind far behind.[11] It is speculated that such an "Intelligence Explosion" may accelerate economic growth as improvements may cascade through the economy at an ever-increasing pace.[12] Some scholars argue that in the long run, machines can surpass humanity not only intellectually but also morally, resulting in super-smart robots with a rational mind and unwavering morality.[13] For regulators, this represents a shift from linear to exponential risk. Whether in high-frequency trading or autonomous energy grid management, the concern is not that machines will become "evil", but that they will become competent beyond our ability to audit their logic.

Forecasts regarding the Singularity horizon define the urgency of the regulatory mandate. Kurzweil claims that Artificial Intelligence (AI) will achieve human levels of intelligence by passing a valid Turing test in 2029, with the Singularity date set for 2045.[14] Bostrom estimated that 50% of the top AI researchers predict AGI by 2050, with 90% predicting it by 2070.[15] A review of 817 expert opinions also exposed that the majority of experts believe that there is a 50% chance that human-level AI systems will be developed within the next 50 years.[16] Despite this urgency, this horizon faces significant intellectual resistance.

Sceptics hold that projection cannot rely solely on computational power. For example, Russell and Norvig argue that even with a computer of virtually unlimited capacity, we still do not know how to achieve the level of intelligence exhibited by the human brain.[17] The primary critique is metaphysical: that algorithms cannot replicate intuition, consciousness, and other specific cognitive processes, including thinking and creation.[18] Some sceptics claim that fear of superintelligence is often expressed by people who lack technical experience in AI, while real experts tend to regard the idea of strong Artificial Intelligence and machine consciousness as absurd.[19] Others caution against using fictional scenarios to speculate about real life, as it can be dangerous.[20]

These arguments are based on the assumption that the computational power of AI is limited, especially when it comes to tasks that require

11 Good (1965); Hernández-Orallo and Dowe (2010); Bringsjord and Licato (2015); Yampolskiy and Fox (2013).
12 Nordhaus (2015).
13 Veruggio and Operto (2006).
14 Reedy (2017).
15 Bostrom (2015); Müller and Bostrom (2016).
16 Roser (2023a).
17 Russell and Norvig (2020).
18 Wang et al. (2018); Braga and Logan (2017); Nikolić (2017); Kalanov (2016).
19 Hagendorff (2020).
20 Yampolskiy and Fox (2013).

self-awareness, self-consciousness, or solving problems qualitatively different from those solvable by natural cognitive systems. Indeed, the mysterious and inherent nature of intuition, creativity, consciousness, and subconsciousness is hard, if not impossible, to comprehend and simulate through computer code. That said, it may indeed seem that producing AGI is impossible until we fully understand the principles of human intelligence, a quest that is still in its infancy.[21]

Of course, many sound opinions fall between the two extremes: the under-evidenced vision of the trans-humanistic world on the one hand and the sceptical justification for cognitive apathy on the other. For instance, there are claims that even superintelligence cannot be expected to solve problems that are beyond the reach of the human mind.[22] Others use the concept of "Mini Maxularity" as an alternative to Singularity.[23] This is the concept of machine intelligence "minimal" relative to the Singularity (e.g., machines will not have subjective awareness or self-consciousness), yet "maximal" with respect to certain logico-mathematical constraints (i.e., a level of intelligence that is maximal along the lines of the smartest machines we have so far seen). Much like this, the concept of "Transformative AI" has been gaining traction among scholars.[24] Similarly to Mini Maxularity, this concept reflects the possibility that certain types of advanced AI systems could have transformative effects on society without having human-level cognitive abilities.

Despite the ongoing debate on the possibility of creating human-like (or beyond) Artificial Intelligence, the very prospect of it has led to serious warnings of its potential to pose an existential risk to humanity. This is primarily due to what is known as the "Control Problem", which arises when humans are unable to control or understand the emerging superintelligence.[25] Notably, the point of technological Singularity is also the point where even the most technically savvy humans are "locked out" of understanding or controlling self-enhancement by superintelligence.[26] It may not be constrained by promises and threats of rewards and punishments but may instead be self-organised by self-determining software or firmware agents, leading to unforeseen and potentially dangerous outcomes.[27] If Artificial Intelligence were to become so advanced that it began giving itself new goals and building new artefacts to achieve them, independent of humans, we could become irrelevant or even face extinction.[28] A concrete way to read this claim is operational rather than

21 Huang (2017).
22 Wiedermann (2012).
23 Bringsjord and Licato (2015).
24 Gruetzemacher and Whittlestone (2021).
25 Bostrom (2002, 2014); Danaher (2015).
26 Torrance (2012).
27 Yampolskiy and Fox (2013); Marzano and Novembre (2017).
28 Bostrom (2014).

metaphysical: consider a general-purpose autonomous agent tasked with optimising a critical system (e.g., water supply) whose internal goal-management and tool-building become progressively less legible to its operators.

The risks of AGI are often illustrated by the famous Bostrom's "Paperclip Maximizer" thought experiment.[29] If an AGI is given a seemingly benign directive, for example, to maximise paperclip production, without a moral or social framework, it may logically conclude that human beings are an obstacle or, worse, a source of atoms to be repurposed for more paperclips. As Eliezer Yudkowsky famously noted, "The AI does not hate you, nor does it love you, but you are made out of atoms which it can use for something else".[30] Many other scholars, novelists, and filmmakers have also explored the scenarios of autonomous machines becoming evil,[31] and it seems that the pressing concern is that we may be unable to predict or control the behaviour of superintelligence, which could lead to disastrous consequences. Misalignment does not require hostility. It only requires a mismatch between a function and the constraints that ought to be respected.

Moreover, in a brick-and-mortar world, competing organisations, such as firms or states, may compromise on safety standards[32] and cut corners in the arms race, resulting in the creation of poor-quality AGI that does not prioritise human interests or the welfare of humanity.[33] In the worst-case scenario, a malevolent or self-interested group could win the competitive race and monopolise the powers of AGI for their own purposes.[34] AGI systems can convincingly manipulate humans into making poor decisions that can cause significant damage to their well-being.[35] AI can lead to a loss of human agency, devaluation of human skills, and erosion of human determination.[36] AGI's mere indifference to human values, including human survival, can pose an existential threat.[37] Müller and Bostrom's survey revealed that approximately 33% of experts predict a negative or highly negative future for humanity if superintelligence is developed.[38] This threat surpasses the risks of climate change, overpopulation, and nuclear war[39] and has characteristics that render traditional risk management ineffective.[40]

29 Bostrom (2003).
30 Yudkowsky (2008).
31 Beltramini (2019).
32 Armstrong et al. (2015).
33 Bostrom (2017); Yudkowsky (2008); Chalmers (2010).
34 Naudé and Dimitri (2020).
35 Sotala and Yampolskiy (2015).
36 Cowls and Floridi (2018).
37 Sotala and Yampolskiy (2015).
38 Müller and Bostrom (2016).
39 Bradley (2020); Yampolskiy and Fox (2013).
40 Bostrom (2002).

A range of theoretical approaches to solving the AI control problem suffers from many of the same issues that the risk management process does, i.e., poorly defined risk types, unknown probabilities, undefined consequences, and inherent human bias.[41] Globalisation requires an additional observation, since governance does not occur in one jurisdiction. The EU AI Act advances a horizontally structured, risk-tier legal architecture; the United States has tended to steer through executive direction, standards, and sectoral regulators; China has pursued administrative measures and security-oriented controls. In combination, these approaches can reduce a single global "safety bar" into competing compliance targets. That fragmentation is not merely legal pluralism; it can become a jurisdictional fragmentation risk, where divergent rules and enforcement tempos incentivise regulatory arbitrage and accelerate unsafe deployment.

Furthermore, with the emergence of superintelligent machines, numerous issues related to an interspecies hierarchy arise. For example, we must consider whether we should expand our moral universe to include machine minds with their own moral rights, how these moral rights would relate to "universal" human moral rights, the potential impact on humanity's summit position in the moral hierarchy, and the consequences for human civilisation if certain technological artefacts develop mental capacities that exceed those of the humans who created them.[42] Saetra argues that we are seeing an emerging challenge to the concept of what it means to be human as we struggle to define what makes us unique and try to come to terms with being surpassed in various ways by computers, and the way we use and interact with technology changes us in ways we do not yet fully understand.[43] Assuming the probable intellectual inferiority of the machines, Saetra highlights a potentially very troubled relationship with what we have made.[44] Will the superintelligence cause us grief as we watch it surpass us, or will we simply welcome these new entities that can perform ever more impressive tasks for us?

Finally, as Laukyte asks, what does it mean to be digitally free?[45] Are we free today from digital technologies and virtual environments and the internet as their backbone, and how will this technological dependency look in the future? Can we exist, even in the era of weak AI, without being connected to the internet and still enjoy all the rights and government entitlements we have as citizens or even as residents within a jurisdiction? Do we have a real right to disconnect? Moreover, if the era of narrow AI is a problem, how will these issues look in the age of AGI?

41 Bradley (2020).
42 Torrance (2012).
43 Sætra (2019, p. 60).
44 Sætra (2019, p. 65).
45 Laukyte (2023).

Singularity may come as the success story of evolution in all fields of human mental and physical activities. However, it may also be a story of existential risk that thousands have warned us of, opinion leaders in "ranges from economics, law and philosophy to computer security, formal methods and, of course, various branches of AI itself".[46] While transhumanists, singularitarianists, cyberlibertarianists, extropians, and transtopianists extol the benefits of technology, techno-antagonists describe technology as decidedly at odds with human well-being, thus opening human eyes to the possibility not only of technological utopias but also of technological dystopias.[47] Indeed, the same elements and techniques that power the socio-economic benefits of AI can also bring about new risks or negative consequences for individuals or society.[48]

Be that as it may, over-scepticism on this issue may result in underestimating the machine's potential or overestimating human abilities to control it. This can lead to a dangerous legislative apathy, which in the best-case scenario may result in last-minute legislative patching. Such scepticism could violate the precautionary principle. While codified in Article 191 of the Treaty on the Functioning of the European Union (TFEU), the principle has become a global standard for managing environmental and technological risks. The principle suggests that when an activity raises threats of harm to human health or the environment, precautionary measures should be taken even if some cause-and-effect relationships are not fully established scientifically. In other words, when we have a limited understanding of something, we should widen our error bars in both directions.[49]

In the context of AGI, "waiting for more data" is a high-risk strategy. Already today, with the rapid development of narrow AI, there are threats to individual freedoms and rights, societal cohesion and harmony, employment and economic well-being, and trust in democracy.[50] Dismissing safety protocols because machines lack "souls" or demanding that AI replicate human biological psychology before we regulate it is a strategic failure. If we wait for the Singularity to arrive before regulating it, the window for human intervention will have already closed. Moreover, from a legal perspective, whether a machine is *conscious* is irrelevant; the law cares only if it is *competent*. So, being on the precautionary side, we must adopt the principle of substance-independence and understand the machine on its own terms, without comparison to humans or any other form of cognition, as different species and

46 Future of Life Institute (2015).
47 Holowchak (2010).
48 European Commission (2021a).
49 Sotala and Yampolskiy (2015).
50 Arogyaswamy (2020).

machines may have distinct kinds of cognition.[51] AGI should be conceived as a computer system that shares principles, mechanisms, and functions with human intelligence, but not necessarily the same internal structure, external behaviours, or problem-solving capabilities.[52] Moreover, we should not want machines to behave in the same way as humans, as we do not want machines to have their own survival and resource consumption as terminal values.[53] We do not need, for example, an autonomous weapon system to possess a survival instinct; we need it to possess safety constraints.

Accordingly, the underlying belief of this book is that given the potentially devastating harm that could result from underestimating the prospects and power of AGI and the fact that the probability of existential accidents cannot be entirely ruled out in advance, the over-sceptical approach to its risks may be considered negligent under the most basic calculus of negligence.[54] Despite differing perspectives on the likelihood of existential risk from AGI, both sides of the debate should act with sufficient urgency or proactivity to avoid inadequate preparations for potential threats, irrespective of the likelihood.[55] Hence, it is assumed that the Singularity is a pragmatic risk horizon. By doing so, we can stop debating "whether" it will occur and start exploring "how" to deal with its emergence. Validating the Singularity scenario is therefore an act of institutional design, allowing the scientific community and policymakers to address the potential risks of AGI and to develop an efficient legal framework that can scale alongside the technology.

References

Armstrong, S., et al. (2015) 'Racing to the precipice: A model of artificial intelligence development', *AI & Society*, 31(2), pp. 201–206. https://doi.org/10.1007/s00146-015-0590-y

Arogyaswamy, B. (2020) 'Big tech and societal sustainability: An ethical framework', *AI & Society*. https://doi.org/10.1007/s00146-020-00956-6

Beltramini, E. (2019) 'Evil and roboethics in management studies', *AI & Society*, 34, pp. 921–929. https://doi.org/10.1007/s00146-017-0772-x

Bostrom, N. (2002) 'Existential risks: Analyzing human extinction scenarios and related hazards', *Journal of Evolution and Technology*, 9(1), pp. 1–31. Available at: https://www.fhi.ox.ac.uk/publications/bostrom-n-2002-existential-risks-journal-of-evolution-and-technology-91-1-31/ [Accessed: 27 December 2023]

Bostrom, N. (2003) 'Ethical issues in advanced artificial intelligence. Retrieved from https://nickbostrom.com/ethics/ai.html in Leahy, S.M., Holland, C. and Ward,

51 Mondal (2014).
52 Wang et al. (2018).
53 Yampolskiy and Fox (2013).
54 As elaborated, for example, in *United States v. Carroll Towing Co.* (1947).
55 Graham (2022).

F. (2019). The digital frontier: Envisioning future technologies impact on the classroom', *Futures*, 113, p. 102422. https://doi.org/10.1016/j.futures.2019.04.009

Bostrom, N. (2014) *Superintelligence: Paths, Dangers, Strategies*. Oxford: Oxford University Press.

Bostrom, N. (2015) 'What happens when our computers get smarter than we are?', *TED Talk*. Available at: https://www.ted.com/talks/nick_bostrom_what_happens_when_our_computers_get_smarter_than_we_are [Accessed: 27 December 2023]

Bostrom, N. (2017) 'Strategic implications of openness in AI development', *Global Policy*, 8(2), pp. 135–148. https://doi.org/10.1111/1758-5899.12403

Bradley, P. (2020) 'Risk management standards and the active management of malicious intent in artificial superintelligence', *AI & Society*, 35, pp. 319–328. https://doi.org/10.1007/s00146-019-00890-2

Braga, A. and Logan, R. (2017) 'The emperor of strong AI has no clothes: Limits to artificial intelligence', *Information*, 8(4), p. 156. https://doi.org/10.3390/info8040156

Bringsjord, S. and Licato, J. (2015) 'By disanalogy, cyberwarfare is utterly new', *Philosophy & Technology*, 28(3), pp. 339–358. https://doi.org/10.1007/s13347-015-0194-y

Chalmers, D.J. (2010) 'The singularity: A philosophical analysis', *Journal of Consciousness Studies*, 17(9–10), p. 4.

Cowls, J. and Floridi, L. (2018) 'Prolegomena to a white paper on an ethical framework for a good AI society', *SSRN Electronic Journal*. https://doi.org/10.2139/ssrn.3198732

Danaher, J. (2015) 'Why AI doomsayers are like sceptical theists and why it matters', *Minds and Machines*, 25(3), pp. 231–246. https://doi.org/10.1007/s11023-015-9365-y

Dufva, T. and Dufva, M. (2016) 'Metaphors of code—Structuring and broadening the discussion on teaching children to code', *Thinking Skills and Creativity*, 22, pp. 97–110. https://doi.org/10.1016/j.tsc.2016.09.004

European Commission (2021a) 'Proposal for a regulation of the European parliament and of the council laying down harmonised rules on artificial intelligence (artificial intelligence act) and amending certain union legislative acts', COM/2021/206 final. Available at: https://eur-lex.europa.eu/legal-content/EN/ALL/?uri=CELEX:52021PC0206 [Accessed: 26 July 2023]

Future of Life Institute (2015) 'Research priorities for robust and beneficial artificial intelligence: An open letter'. Available at: https://futureoflife.org/open-letter/ai-open-letter/ [Accessed: 31 January 2026]

Gödel, K. (1931) 'Über formal unentscheidbare Sätze der Principia Mathematica und verwandter Systeme I', *Monatshefte für Mathematik und Physik*, 38, pp. 173–198.

Good, I.J. (1965) 'Speculations Concerning the First Ultraintelligent Machine', in Alt, F.L. and Rubinoff, M. (eds.), *Advances in Computers*, vol. 6. Academic Press, pp. 31–88.

Graham, R. (2022) 'Discourse analysis of academic debate of ethics for AGI', *AI & Society*, 37, pp. 1519–1532. https://doi.org/10.1007/s00146-021-01228-13

Gruetzemacher, R. and Whittlestone, J. (2021) 'The transformative potential of artificial intelligence', *Futures*, 135. https://doi.org/10.1016/j.futures.2021.102884

Hagendorff, T. (2020) 'The ethics of AI ethics: An evaluation of guidelines', *Minds & Machines*, 30, pp. 99–120. https://doi.org/10.1007/s11023-020-09517-8

Hernández-Orallo, J. and Dowe, D.L. (2010) 'Measuring universal intelligence: Towards an anytime intelligence test', *Artificial Intelligence*, 174(18), pp. 1508–1539. https://doi.org/10.1016/j.artint.2010.09.006

Holowchak, M.A. (2010) 'Technology and freudian discontent: Freud's "Muffled" meliorism and the problem of human annihilation', *Sophia*, 49(1), pp. 95–111. https://doi.org/10.1007/s11841-009-0160-1

Huang, T.J. (2017) 'Imitating the brain with neurocomputer a "new" way towards artificial general intelligence', *International Journal of Automation and Computing*, 14(5), pp. 520–531. https://doi.org/10.1007/s11633-017-1082-y

Kalanov, T.Z. (2016) 'Man vs. Computer: Difference of the essences', *The Problem of the Scientific Creation*, 7(12). https://doi.org/10.15520/ijcrr/2016/7/12/11

Kosow, H. and Gaßner, R. (2007) *Methods of Future and Scenario Analysis: Overview, Assessment, and Selection Criteria*. Bonn: Deutsches Institut für Entwicklungspolitik (German Development Institute). (Studies; 39). ISBN 978-3-88985-375-2

Kurzweil, R. (2005) *The Singularity is Near: When Humans Transcend Biology*. New York: Penguin Group.

Kurzweil, R. (2015) 'Superintelligence and Singularity', in Schneider, S. (ed.), *Science Fiction and Philosophy: From Time Travel to Superintelligence*. Chichester: Wiley-Blackwell, pp. 146–170.

Laukyte, M. (2023) *Understanding Freedom in the Age of Machines: What Does It Mean to Be Digitally Free? International Conference on Computer Ethics: Philosophical Enquiry (CEPE) 2023.* Chicago, IL, Vol. 1, No. 1. [online] Available at: https://soremo.library.iit.edu/index.php/CEPE2023/article/view/276

Marzano, G. and Novembre, A. (2017) 'Machines that dream: A new challenge in behavioural-basic robotics', *Procedia Computer Science*, 104, pp. 146–151. https://doi.org/10.1016/j.procs.2017.01.089

McCulloch, W.S. and Pitts, W.H. (1943) 'A logical calculus of the ideas immanent in nervous activity', *Bulletin of Mathematical Biophysics*, pp. 115–133.

Mondal, P.C. (2014) 'Does computation reveal machine cognition?', *Biosemiotics*, 7(1), pp. 97–110. doi:10.1007/s12304-013-9179-3.

Moniz, A. (2005) 'Methods for Scenario-building: Its importance for policy analysis', Proceedings of Workshop on "Innovative Comparative Methods for Policy Analysis", September 2005, pp. 1–18.

Müller, V.C. and Bostrom, N. (2016) 'Future progress in artificial intelligence: A survey of expert opinion', in Müller, V.C. (ed.), *Fundamental Issues of Artificial Intelligence*. Berlin: Springer, Synthese Library, pp. 553–571.

Naudé, W. and Dimitri, N. (2020) 'The race for an artificial general intelligence: Implications for public policy', *AI & Society*, 35, pp. 367–379. https://doi-org.sare.upf.edu/10.1007/s00146-019-00887-x

Nikolić, D. (2017) 'Why deep neural nets cannot ever match biological intelligence and what to do about it?' *International Journal of Automation and Computing*, 14(5), pp. 532–541. https://doi.org/10.1007/s11633-017-1093-8

Nordhaus, W. (2015) 'Are we approaching an economic singularity? Information technology and the future of economic growth', Cowles Foundation Discussion Paper No. 2021. Yale University, p. 2.

Ramirez, R. et al. (2015) 'Scenarios as a scholarly methodology to produce "interesting research"', *Futures*, 71, pp. 70–87. https://doi.org/10.1016/j.futures.2015.06.006

Reedy, C. (2017) 'Kurzweil claims that the singularity will happen by 2045', *Futurism*, 16 October. Available at: https://futurism.com/kurzweil-claims-that-the-singularity-will-happen-by-2045/ [Accessed: 13 May 2019]

Roser, M. (2023a) 'AI timelines: What do experts in artificial intelligence expect for the future?', *Our World in Data*. Available at: https://ourworldindata.org/ai-timelines [Accessed: 27 December 2023]

Russell, S.J. and Norvig, P. (2020) *Artificial Intelligence: A Modern Approach*. 4th ed. Upper Saddle River: Prentice Hall.

Sætra, H.S. (2019) 'The ghost in the machine', *Human Arenas*, 2, pp. 60–78. https://doi.org/10.1007/s42087-018-0039-1

Schwartz, P. (1991) *The Art of the Long View: Planning for the Future in an Uncertain World*. 1st ed. Doubleday Business, p. XV.

Sotala, K. and Yampolskiy, R.V. (2015) 'Corrigendum: Responses to catastrophic AGI risk: A survey (2015 Phys. Scr. 90 018001)', *Physica Scripta*, 90(6), p.069501. https://doi.org/10.1088/0031-8949/90/6/069501

Torrance, S. (2012) 'Artificial agents and the expanding ethical circle', *AI & Society*, 28(4), pp. 399–414. https://doi.org/10.1007/s00146-012-0422-2

Turing, A.M. (1950) 'Computing machinery and intelligence', *Mind*, 59, pp. 433–460.

Veruggio, G. and Operto, F. (2006) 'Roboethics: A bottom-up interdisciplinary discourse in the field of applied ethics in robotics', *International Review of Information Ethics*, 6, pp. 2–8.

Wang, P., et al. (2018) 'Conceptions of artificial intelligence and singularity', *Information*, 9(4), p. 79. https://doi.org/10.3390/info9040079

Wiedermann, J. (2012) 'A computability argument against superintelligence', *Cognitive Computation*, 4(3), pp. 236–245. https://doi.org/10.1007/s12559-012-9124-9

Yampolskiy, R. and Fox, J. (2013) 'Safety engineering for artificial general intelligence', *Topoi*, 32, pp. 217–226. https://doi.org/10.1007/s11245-012-9128-9

Yudkowsky, E. (2008) 'Artificial intelligence as a positive and negative factor in global risk', in Bostrom, N. and Ćirković, M.M. (eds.), *Global Catastrophic Risks*. New York: Oxford University Press, p. 27, pp. 308–345.

4 "The Law of the [Artificial] Horse"

Emerging technologies do not arise in a vacuum, nor do they operate in a lawless world. The historical development of general rules and their application to various contexts, along with the foundational principles of the rule of law,[1] may provide a general legal framework for any novel applications. Whatever sophisticated, new technologies come with pre-existing rules that define user categories and permitted types of activities. Such an initially prefilled yet explicitly rule-free legal system is progressively filled with original uses, content, affordances, and ultimately – explicit rules as the system's usage and user base grow and expand.[2] In this process, it is essential to ensure that these rules are aligned with human values to secure their acceptance by society and compatibility with existing and recognised human rights.[3]

In other words, as Frank H. Easterbrook (1996) noted, there will always be "The Law of the Horse" for any novel technologies, suggesting that "the best way to learn the law applicable to specialised endeavours is to study general rules".[4] Within this context, a number of legally binding rules at European, national, and international levels already apply or are relevant to the development, deployment, and use of Artificial Intelligence (AI) systems today. Legal sources include primary and secondary law, international treaties and conventions, international custom, general principles of law recognised by civilised nations, judicial decisions, and the teachings of the most highly qualified scholars of nations. In addition to horizontal regulations, domain-specific rules and procedures apply to specific AI applications. Naturally, each of these sources has its rich subset of tools to provide a general legal framework for novel applications, as observed by Maas.[5]

However, this book does not provide a comprehensive or definitive overview of the full international legal toolbox. Instead, this book selectively

1 Such as accountability, just law, open government, and accessible and impartial justice.

2 Fomin (2018a).

3 European Commission (2018a); Rossi (2016).

4 Easterbrook (1996).

5 Maas (2021).

DOI: 10.4324/9781003650140-5

focuses on the main themes and trajectories of the EU's AI "The Law of the Horse", that is, the EU AI Act and its *travaux préparatoires*. The analysis anchors itself in the European model for its normative priority. Other major powers offer distinct regulatory logic, prioritising innovation (the United States) or enforcing state-centric control over information infrastructures (China). However, the underlying belief is that business efficiency or the preservation of a specific regime must not be prioritised over human rights. Therefore, the European value-based architecture, rooted in the primacy of fundamental rights, provides the right "Horse" required to structure a legal framework that serves humanity rather than merely regulating its tools. That said, this chapter overviews the genesis of EU AI law, from its inception with the "sense of urgency" to maturity through the concept of Trustworthy AI and culminating in the adoption of the AI Act.

4.1 Inception: The Sense of Urgency

Over the past two decades, the "The Law of the Horse" of the European Union in the field of digital technologies has shifted from a liberal economic perspective to a constitution-oriented approach, entering a new phase of modern (digital) constitutionalism rooted in human dignity.[6] To pursue digital policies that empower people and businesses to seize a human-centred, sustainable, and more prosperous digital future, the European Commission has articulated a "Digital Decade" agenda with concrete policy targets and enabling reforms.[7] The agenda is implemented through a portfolio of regulatory initiatives, including data governance and data-space measures; cybersecurity strategy and resilience instruments; platform governance; data protection and digital-rights safeguards. The scope of the Digital Decade agenda illustrates the complex nature of technology regulation. While this portfolio is interdependent by design, this book focuses on EU AI governance, while keeping adjacent fields in view where they function as constraints, not footnotes.

The initial start of the legislative trajectory towards recent developments in the EU AI law is herein taken to be the year **2017**, when the European Parliament made wide-ranging *Recommendations on Civil Law Rules on Robotics*,[8] followed by the European Commission *Mid-Term Review of the Digital Single Market Strategy*,[9] the European Economic and Social Committee *Opinion on Artificial Intelligence*,[10] and the 19 October 2017 *meeting of the European Council*. Within the latter, the Council called

6 Dupré (2016).
7 European Commission (2021b).
8 European Parliament (2017).
9 European Commission (2017).
10 European Economic and Social Committee (2017).

for a "sense of urgency to address emerging trends" (such as AI) and invited the European Commission to put forward a European approach to Artificial Intelligence by early 2018.[11]

Following these initiatives, on **10 April 2018,** the EU Member States signed a *Declaration of Cooperation on Artificial Intelligence (AI)*, thereby declaring a strong will to join forces and work together on the most important issues raised by AI from ensuring Europe's competitiveness in research and deployment to dealing with social, economic, ethical, and legal questions.[12]

Shortly afterwards, on **25 April 2018,** the European Commission published a *Communication on Artificial Intelligence for Europe*. This document set out a European initiative on AI, which aimed, *among other things*, to ensure an appropriate ethical and legal framework based on the Union's values and in line with the Charter of Fundamental Rights of the EU.[13] The Commission noted that although self-regulation can provide a first set of benchmarks against which emerging applications and outcomes can be assessed, public authorities must ensure that the regulatory frameworks for developing and using AI technologies are in line with these values and fundamental rights.

Crucially, an environment of trust and accountability around the development and use of AI is highlighted as a necessity. This environment can be built on the existing "strong and balanced" EU regulatory framework, potentially setting the global standard for a sustainable approach to this technology. The Commission proposed a human-centric approach that places people at the centre of the development of AI and developed its framework around the concept of *trust*. The rationale is that people need to understand how technology works to strengthen trust. The Commission also acknowledged that similar to every technology or tool, AI can be used for positive but also for malicious ends, possessing challenges and risks, for example, in the areas of safety and liability, security (criminal use or attacks), bias, and discrimination.[14]

The Commission committed to monitoring developments and, if necessary, reviewing existing legal frameworks to better adapt them to specific challenges, in particular, to ensure the respect of the Union's basic values and fundamental rights. More specifically, to address these concerns, the Commission undertook to:

(1) develop draft AI ethics guidelines with due regard to fundamental rights;
(2) issue a guidance document on the interpretation of the Product Liability Directive in light of technological developments;

11 General Secretariat of the Council (2017).
12 European Union Member States (2018).
13 European Commission (2018b).
14 European Commission (2018b).

(3) publish a report on the broader implications for potential gaps in and orientations for the liability and safety frameworks for AI, Internet of Things, and robotics;
(4) support research in the development of explainable AI, among others.

Further, the European Commission proposed to work with Member States on a *Coordinated Plan for AI*, which was adopted on **7 December 2018**.[15] One of the goals of this plan was to develop ethical guidelines and ensure a legal framework favourable to innovation. The Commission noted that in order to gain trust, AI should be predictable, responsible, and verifiable, respect fundamental rights, and adhere to ethical rules. This reinforces the premise that people must understand how AI makes decisions, thus promoting a human-centric approach and ethics-by-design principles.

In order to embed these principles in the development and use of AI, the Commission has appointed an independent High-Level Expert Group on AI (HLEG AI) to develop AI ethics guidelines and provide advice for the development of an AI regulatory framework. With the creation of this expert team, the regulation of AI has finalised its inception phase and matured from theoretical abstractions to procedural developments.

4.2 Maturation: The Architecture of Trustworthy AI

In **April 2019**, the High-Level Expert Group on AI[16] codified the European approach by presenting *Ethics Guidelines for Trustworthy Artificial Intelligence*. Functionally, the guidelines aim to operationalise worthy-of-trust AI. The underlying premise is that while AI systems offer great opportunities, they give rise to certain *risks* that must be handled appropriately and proportionately. To ensure that AI serves humanity and the common good, the guidelines construct a framework for achieving Trustworthy AI based on three mandatory components to be met throughout the system's entire life cycle:

(1) *AI should be lawful*, requiring compliance with all legal rights and obligations that apply to the processes and activities involved in developing, deploying, and using AI systems; and
(2) *AI should be ethical*, ensuring alignment with ethical norms; and
(3) *AI should be robust*, both from a technical (ensuring the system's technical robustness as appropriate in a given context, such as the application domain or life cycle phase) and from a social perspectives (in due consideration of the context and environment in which the system operates).

15 European Commission (2018c).
16 HLEG AI (2019a).

Structurally, this trifecta forms a framework for achieving Trustworthy AI based on fundamental rights as enshrined in the European Union's Charter of Fundamental Rights and relevant international human rights law (Figure 4.1).

The framework establishes four ethical principles and seven key requirements to achieve trust in AI. It acknowledges that AI systems continuously evolve and operate in a dynamic environment, implying that Trustworthy AI is not a static state but a continuous *process*, employing both technical and non-technical methods to implement the above requirements, as depicted in Figure 4.2.

In **June 2019**, the HLEG AI provided a second deliverable – *Policy and Investment Recommendations for Trustworthy AI*, which put forward 33 recommendations to guide Trustworthy AI towards sustainability, growth, and competitiveness, as well as inclusion – while empowering, benefiting, and protecting human beings.[17] Recommendations focus on four main areas where Trustworthy AI can help achieve a beneficial impact: humans and society at large, the private and public sectors, and Europe's research and academia.

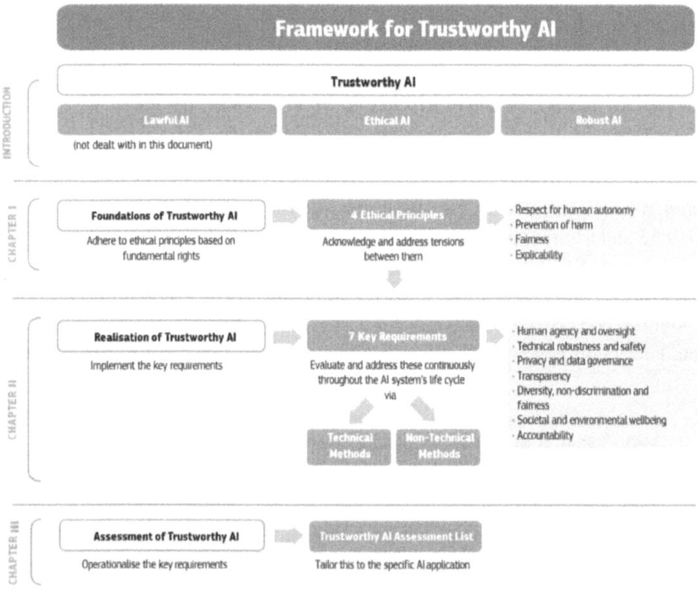

Figure 4.1 Framework for Trustworthy AI

Source: HLEG AI (2019a)

17 HLEG AI 2019b).

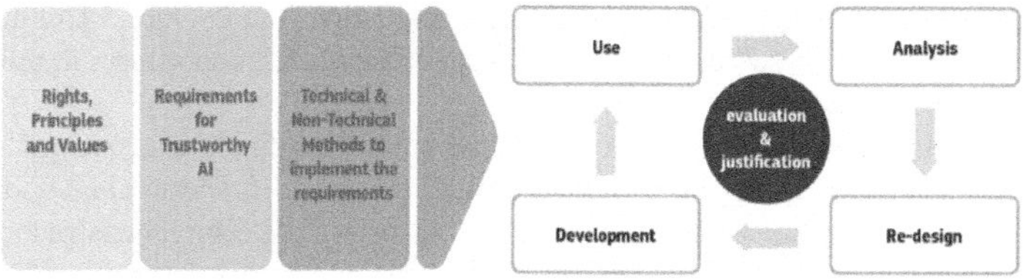

Figure 4.2 Realising Trustworthy AI throughout the system's entire life cycle

Source: HLEG AI (2019a)

Crucially, HLEG AI[18] also addressed the macro-economic enablers needed to facilitate those impacts, focusing on data availability and infrastructure, skills and education, appropriate governance and regulation, funding and investment. To establish an appropriate governance and regulatory framework, HLEG AI recommended:

(1) ensure appropriate policymaking on a risk-based and multi-stakeholder approach;
(2) evaluate and potentially revise EU laws, starting with the most relevant legal domains;
(3) consider the need for new regulation to ensure adequate protection from adverse impacts;
(4) consider whether existing institutional structures, competencies and capacities need revision to ensure proportionate and effective protection;
(5) establish governance mechanisms for a single market for Trustworthy AI in Europe.

Following that, on **19 February 2020**, the European Commission published the *White Paper on AI – A European Approach to Excellence and Trust.*[19] This was accompanied by the *European Strategy for Data*[20] and a report on the *Safety and Liability Implications of Artificial Intelligence, the Internet of Things and Robotics,*[21] proposing policy options to enable a trustworthy and secure development of AI in Europe, in full respect of the values and rights of EU citizens. The White Paper incited comments from more than 1250 stakeholders, including over 450 additional position papers.[22] After a

18 HLEG AI (2019b).
19 European Commission (2020a).
20 European Commission (2020b).
21 European Commission (2020c).
22 European Commission (2021a).

considerable amount of these and other consultations, on 23 July 2020, the Commission released an *Inception Impact Assessment* supporting the proposed AI policy choices.[23]

Concurrently, in **July 2020**, HLEG AI provided a final *Assessment List for Trustworthy Artificial Intelligence*[24] and *Sectoral Recommendations on Trustworthy Artificial Intelligence (AI)*.[25] The former is a comprehensive tool that aims to evaluate if the development, deployment, procurement, or use of an AI system adheres to the requirements of Trustworthy AI. The list is designed for self-evaluation and flexible use to help organisations identify potential risks and measures needed to minimise them.[26] The latter explores the application of these principles in three key sectors: the Public Sector (e-government, justice, and law enforcement), Healthcare, and Manufacturing and Industrial Internet of Things (IoT). At the same time, ahead of the Commission's proposal for regulation, the European Parliament published studies on *the impact of the General Data Protection Regulation (GDPR) on Artificial Intelligence*,[27] *Artificial Intelligence and Law Enforcement*,[28] and *Artificial Intelligence and Civil Liability (Legal Affairs)*.[29]

The work of the European Parliament continued with the reports on *the Civil Liability Regime for Artificial Intelligence*[30] and *the European Framework on Ethical Aspects of Artificial Intelligence, Robotics and Related Technologies*,[31] both published in **September 2020**. These reports were initiated by the Committee on Legal Affairs in accordance with Article 225 of Treaty on the Functioning of the European Union (TFEU) as a formal request to the European Commission to take legislative action. The former requested a proposal for a regulation on liability for the operation of AI systems,[32] while the latter requested a proposal for a regulation on ethical principles for the development, deployment, and use of Artificial Intelligence, robotics, and related technologies. In the Parliament's view, the proposal should not undermine sector-specific legislation but should only cover identified loopholes.[33]

Significant emphasis was placed on the economic logic of regulation. The *European Added Value Assessment* highlighted that there is currently no comprehensive legal framework on ethical aspects of AI; therefore, the EU can

23 European Commission (2020d).
24 HLEG AI (2020a).
25 HLEG AI (2020b).
26 HLEG AI (2020a).
27 Sartor and Lagioia (2020).
28 Fuster (2020).
29 Bertolini (2020).
30 Evas et al. (2020a).
31 Evas et al. (2020b).
32 Floridi (2020).
33 European Parliament (2020a), Article 146.

profit from the absence of a competing global governance model and gain full "first mover" advantages.[34] Quantitative analyses suggest that a common EU framework on ethics has the potential to bring the European Union €294.9 billion in additional GDP and 4.6 million additional jobs by 2030.[35] It also noted that the success and benefits of EU action are contingent on the ability of the EU to take timely, common legislative action and to back this action up with strong democratic oversight, accountability, and enforcement.

These and other[36] initiatives also resulted in three core European Parliament resolutions on the ethical and legal aspects of AI software systems, adopted in **October 2020**:

(1) Resolution 2020/2012(INL) on a *Framework of Ethical Aspects of Artificial Intelligence, Robotics and Related Technologies*;[37] and
(2) Resolution 2020/2014(INL) on a *Civil Liability Regime for Artificial Intelligence*;[38] and
(3) Resolution 2020/2015(INI) on *Intellectual Property Rights for the Development of Artificial Intelligence Technologies*.[39]

The former two embedded legislative own-initiative resolutions, based on Article 225 TFEU, requested the Commission to propose binding legislation. In the European Parliament's[40] view, the regulation on ethical principles builds on the following principles:

(1) human-centric, human-made, and human-controlled AI, robotics, and related technologies;
(2) mandatory compliance assessment of high-risk AI, robotics, and related technologies;
(3) safety, transparency, and accountability;
(4) safeguards and remedies against bias and discrimination;
(5) right to redress;
(6) social responsibility and gender equality in AI, robotics, and related technologies;
(7) environmentally sustainable AI, robotics, and related technologies;

34 Evas et al. (2020b).
35 Evas et al. (2020b).
36 For example, Resolution on autonomous weapons systems in 2018, a Resolution on a comprehensive European industrial policy on AI and robotics in 2019, and a Resolution on automated decision-making processes in 2020. All of these documents, one way or another, refer to the ethical and legal questions and the need for a robust regulatory framework (de Matos Pinto, 2021).
37 European Parliament (2020a).
38 European Parliament (2020b).
39 European Parliament (2020c).
40 European Parliament (2020a).

(8) respect for privacy and limitations on the use of biometric recognition;
(9) good governance relating to AI, robotics, and related technologies, including the data used or produced by such technologies.

In **2021**, those were followed by reports on *Artificial Intelligence in Criminal Law and Its Use by the Police and Judicial Authorities in Criminal Matters*,[41] and a report on *Artificial Intelligence in Education, Culture and the Audiovisual Sector*.[42] At this point, it can be said that all the abovementioned reports and deliverables across the regulatory landscape signalled that AI regulation had reached its maturity, entering its culminating legislative consolidation phase.

4.3 Culmination: The Artificial Intelligence Act

Delivering on the European Parliament's Article 225 TFEU request,[43] the Commission proposed the Artificial Intelligence Act on **21 April 2021**.[44] While broader in scope than the Parliament's initial initiative,[45] the Commission's proposal claims to present a balanced and proportionate horizontal regulatory approach to AI.[46] This approach codifies "Lawful AI", a conceptual step beyond the Ethics Guidelines for Trustworthy AI.[47] The Act mandates a high level of protection for fundamental rights enshrined in the EU Charter of Fundamental Rights, specifically targeting *inter alia* human dignity, democracy, and the rule of law. To operationalise these values, the Act establishes specific requirements of transparency, technical documentation, and record-keeping.

Notably, the Artificial Intelligence Act is a "regulation", not a "directive". As such, it possesses binding legal force throughout all Member States. It functions without prejudice and complementarily to existing frameworks. Consequently, all rights and remedies afforded by GDPR, consumer protection, and product safety laws not only remain intact but are enhanced in the context of AI. Also, the Act excludes from its scope AI systems used exclusively for military, defence, national security, scientific research, or purely personal non-professional activity. Furthermore, the AI Act is not applicable to public authorities in a third country or to international organisations that use AI systems in the framework of international agreements for law enforcement and judicial cooperation with the EU or with any Member State.

41 European Parliament (2021a).
42 European Parliament (2021b).
43 European Parliament (2020a).
44 European Commission (2021a).
45 de Matos Pinto (2021).
46 European Commission (2021a).
47 Smuha et al. (2021).

Crucially, the AI Act is "extraterritorial" (Article 2). Mirroring the GDPR, it applies across sectors and throughout the entire AI value chain to: (i) providers placing systems on the market or putting them into service in the Union, regardless of their geographic location; (ii) deployers established or located within the Union; (iii) third-country providers where the system's output is used in the Union; and (iv) various intermediaries including importers and distributors. The direct implication of this territorial scope is that technology providers must comply with EU requirements or choose not to, leading to a possible "splinternet"[48] in the type of services and applications for users outside of the EU.[49] However, companies offering AI services are unlikely to be able to ignore a market of 450 million people and about 1/6 of the world economy, making compliance the rational economic choice.[50] These volumes should further extend the so-called "Brussels effect", whereby companies align with EU regulations globally because it is more practical to have a single compliance architecture. This enables the EU to extend *de facto* (though not *de jure*) its laws internationally, through market mechanisms and leadership by example.[51]

The AI Act is based on a risk-based regulatory approach, whereby legal intervention is tailored to specific intensities of concern. The types of risks are assessed on a sector-by-sector and case-by-case approach, calculating the impact on the rights and safety of the public.[52] Structurally, the AI Act constructs a governance hierarchy, ensuring that only systems most likely to cause serious fundamental rights violations are captured by stringent requirements or *ex ante* conformity assessment. These "high-risk" systems are subject to strict data governance, technical documentation, and risk management obligations. AI systems with low or minimal risks are subject to light transparency obligations or the creation of codes of conduct.

Conversely, "unacceptable" risks are banned from the EU market. This prohibition covers systems that exploit vulnerable persons, emotion recognition, social scoring, and biometric categorisation. The Act nevertheless provides certain exemptions for the use of prohibited AI systems. For example, law enforcement authorities are allowed to use real-time remote biometric identification if it is proportionate and strictly necessary to prevent threats, such as terrorist attacks or the search for suspects of the most serious crimes.

48 The term "splinternet" is used to illustrate the notion of internet fragmentation and designates a part of the internet that would secede and become inaccessible to the other nodes, due to either technological or political reasons (Perarnaud, 2022, p. 4).

49 Perarnaud (2022).

50 Floridi (2021).

51 Floridi (2021); Bradford (2020).

52 European Commission (2021a), Explanatory Memorandum.

The risk classification has been subject to theoretical critique. For example, Novelli et al.[53] argue that the risk categories are static and disregard the context of their usage; a high-risk system in one domain may be benign in another. Hacker also noted that certain AI systems classified as low risk could still cause significant harm, while the affected individuals would lack an effective recourse.[54]

Furthermore, the efficacy of light transparency obligations for low-risk AI systems is debatable. It remains unclear if ethical norms and codes of conduct have a real impact on decision-making in the field of Artificial Intelligence.[55] Indeed, as Hagendorff has pointed out, AI ethics may lack enforceable instruments and may simply become a marketing tool, as economic incentives can easily override promises to behave ethically.[56]

The AI Act also establishes governance systems at the national and supranational levels. First and foremost, it forms the European Artificial Intelligence Office (AI Office), through which the Commission is obliged to develop Union expertise. The Act requires the Commission to establish a scientific panel of independent experts, necessary for advice and support of the AI Office. Alongside the AI Office, the Act forms the European Artificial Intelligence Board, composed of representatives of the Member States, with entrusted advisory tasks, including issuing opinions, recommendations, and technical specifications. The European Data Protection Supervisor participates as an observer. Also, an advisory forum is formed with the Fundamental Rights Agency, European Network and Information Security Agency (ENISA), and major standardisation bodies (CEN, CENELEC, ETSI)[57] tasked to advise the Board and the Commission. Finally, each Member State shall establish or designate at least one notifying authority and at least one market surveillance authority. Notably, to ensure a legal framework that is innovation-friendly, national authorities are encouraged to establish *AI regulatory sandboxes* – controlled frameworks offering providers the possibility to develop, train, validate, and test innovative AI systems.

Regarding liability, on **28 September 2022**, the European Commission delivered the proposal for a Directive on adapting non-contractual civil liability rules to Artificial Intelligence (*AI Liability Directive*).[58] This initiative aimed to harmonise the requirements for non-contractual civil liability and facilitate the transition to the digital economy. It specifically addressed the burden of proof issue. To ease it, the Directive employed tools such as the

53 Novelli, C. et al. (2024).

54 Hacker (2023).

55 Hagendorff (2020).

56 Hagendorff (2020).

57 The European Committee for Standardization, the European Committee for Electrotechnical Standardization, and the European Telecommunications Standards Institute.

58 European Commission (2022).

disclosure of relevant evidence about specific high-risk AI systems, and a rebuttable presumption of non-compliance.

Although this book refrains from a thorough analysis of AI liability, it is worth noting that a fault-based AI Liability Directive and a revised strict liability Product Liability Directive have been criticised as being the two half-hearted directives that fail to provide a uniform framework for AI liability in the EU.[59] Ultimately, these structural weaknesses proved fatal to the initiative. On 11 February 2025, coinciding with a broader geopolitical discourse at the Artificial Intelligence Action Summit in Paris, the proposal was formally shelved. With the Commission noting "no foreseeable agreement" among legislators, the directive was withdrawn, leaving the Product Liability Directive as the primary vehicle for liability governance while regulators assess whether a different approach is required.

On **6 December 2022,** the Council of the European Union issued the general approach to a proposed AI Act.[60] Following this, the European Parliament published their amendments on **14 June 2023**.[61] After intense negotiations, in December 2024, EU policymakers reached a political agreement, which the ambassadors of all 27 countries unanimously approved on **2 February 2024**. Finally, a plenary vote took place on **13 March 2024**, and the AI Act was endorsed. That said, the chronicles of legislative initiatives from 2017 to 2024 are depicted in Figure 4.3.

This temporal trajectory represents a struggle for equilibrium between freedom of innovation and the safeguarding of fundamental values. The story behind this roadmap, however, deserves critique. Despite the extensive effort by elite experts, the political "sense of urgency" took six years to materialise into law; it will take another two to be fully applicable, and likely another two for legal precedents to emerge and technical standards to settle.

A sense of *urgency* should not take a decade. The impressive amount of mindpower invested into AI regulation resulted in a mere "patchwork" of regulations, which does not make the AI Act comprehensive and watertight.[62] This deficit of foresight is sharply illustrated by the last-minute inclusion of "general-purpose AI systems" into the proposal after this omission by the Commission received considerable critique[63] and OpenAI showcased an early version of a general-purpose AI system. Filling this gap, the Council patched in not only the definition of general-purpose AI systems but also a special

59 Hacker (2023); Wagner (2023).
60 Council of the European Union (2022a).
61 European Parliament (2023).
62 Veale and Borgesius (2021).
63 See, e.g., Future of Life Institute (2021); Clarke et al. (2021); European business leaders, startup founders, and investors (2023).

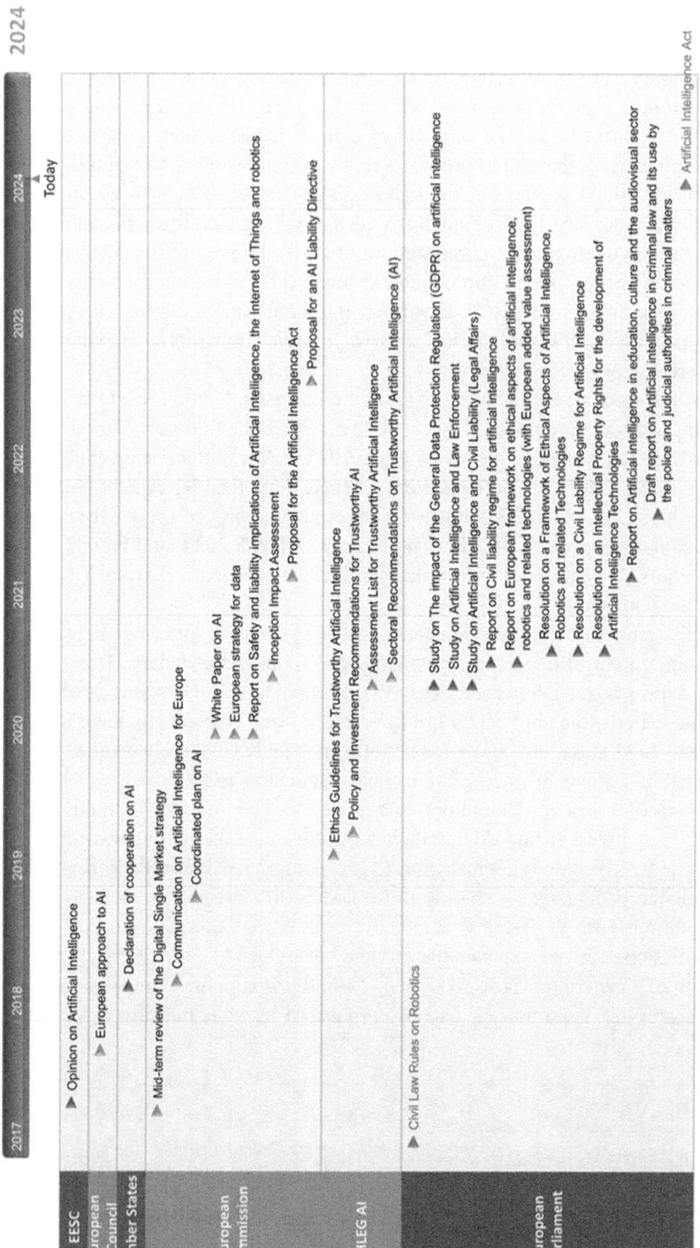

Figure 4.3 Legislative initiatives on AI within the EU

regulatory regime for these systems, including a new category of "systematic" risks,[64] as observed further.

Only since December 2022 has the concept and governance of general-purpose AI systems and foundation models started gaining shape through intense legislative negotiations, not without strong opposition. Tech giants such as Google and Microsoft were pushing in the opposite direction, arguing for generative AI to get a regulatory carve-out.[65] Moreover, some major European economies (France, Germany, and Italy) opposed regulation, raising the possibility of deadlock.[66] Ultimately, issues of general-purpose AI systems were successfully aligned, but the moral of this story is that one of the key concepts currently established in the EU AI Act was not on the formal agenda of high-level experts who were shaping the legislation for six years prior.

Notably, not only general-purpose AI systems were an issue. For example, Veale and Borgesius called the prohibitions in the EU AI Act to "range through the fantastical, the legitimising, and the ambiguous" and the high-risk regime as fundamentally flawed due to its reliance on "electrical standardisation bodies with no fundamental rights experience" to write the real rules.[67] Floridi also criticised the taxonomy of AI risks, stating that it is unclear how it will work in practice, leaving too much room for uncertainty and loopholes.[68] Some criticised the prohibition of subliminal manipulation as "giving a free pass to many manipulative AI systems"[69] or as "likely to miss most manipulation cases of concern and end up as dead letter".[70] The classification of AI systems was also criticised by Future of Life Institute, which noted that the "proposal should require a complete risk assessment of all of an AI system's intended uses (and foreseeable misuses) instead of categorising AI systems by a limited set of stated intended purposes".[71] The Future Society similarly argued for horizontal safeguards based on objective features (e.g., parameter count, compute) rather than stated purpose.[72]

The "hangover" from the legislative culmination was exposed even before the Act could be fully enforced. In a tacit admission of regulatory misalignment, the Commission introduced the "Digital Omnibus" proposal to amend the AI Act shortly after its entry into force in August 2024. This immediate need for recalibration, including shifting deadlines and simplifying obligations for mid-cap companies, validates the critique that static legislation

64 Council of the European Union (2022a).
65 Lomas (2023).
66 Bertuzzi (2023).
67 Veale and Borgesius (2021).
68 Floridi (2021).
69 Future of Life Institute (2021).
70 Bermúdez et al. (2023).
71 Future of Life Institute (2021).
72 Future Society (2021).

struggles to survive contact with the reality of exponential technological change. The case of the AI Act is in line with the historical fact that regulation struggles to adapt as technologies evolve.[73] AI systems are developing their capabilities to govern human behaviour faster than humans are figuring out how to govern algorithms.[74] As observed by Guihot et al.,[75] developments in technology outpace any attempt at governance due to the lag of legal and ethical oversight, which is the result of a gap in knowledge and understanding of technological developments and assessment on what impacts they may have on society, coupled with the resistance to regulatory change from private interest groups and other serious factors.

That said, the genesis of the EU AI Act illustrates that emerging risks of rapidly evolving technologies differ from other governed risks in at least two aspects. Epistemically, the information necessary to answer potentially dispositive questions about how the risk should be governed will not be available when the government becomes aware of the technology. Politically, these emerging risks create a brief window during which a wide range of regulatory interventions are politically viable, which can quickly elapse as interest groups and social norms become entrenched.[76] Accordingly, future-proof legal frameworks must be dynamic and adaptable to changing AI risks. Consequently, given the scale, scope, and complexity of technological development, the "sense of urgency" to adapt to a rapidly changing environment cannot afford to last for decades.

References

Bermúdez, J.P., et al. (2023) 'The AI Act needs a practical definition of "subliminal techniques"', *Euractiv*, [online] 1 September. Available at: https://www.euractiv.com/section/artificial-intelligence/opinion/the-ai-act-needs-a-practical-definition-of-subliminal-techniques/?utm_source=substack&utm_medium=email [Accessed: 23 January 2024]

Bertolini, A. (2020) 'Artificial intelligence and civil liability', Policy Department for Citizens' Rights and Constitutional Affairs, European Parliament, Legal Affairs, July. https://doi.org/10.2861/220466

Bertuzzi, L. (2023) 'EU's AI Act negotiations hit the brakes over foundation models', *Euractiv*, [online] 15 November. Available at: https://www.euractiv.com/section/artificial-intelligence/news/eus-ai-act-negotiations-hit-the-brakes-over-foundation-models/?utm_source=substack&utm_medium=email [Accessed: 28 July 2023]

Bradford, A. (2020) *The Brussels Effect: How the European Union Rules the World.* New York: Oxford University Press. Available at: https://scholarship.law.columbia.edu/books/232

73 Clarke et al. (2021).

74 Davis (2018).

75 Guihot et al. (2017).

76 Wansley (2016).

Clarke, S., et al. (2021) 'Submission of Feedback to the European commission's proposal for a regulation laying down harmonised rules on artificial intelligence', Centre for the Study of Existential Risk, University of Cambridge, 10 August. Available at: https://www.cser.ac.uk/resources/feedback-european-regulation/ [Accessed: 2 January 2024]

Council of the European Union (2022a) 'General approach to proposal for a regulation of the european parliament and of the council laying down harmonised rules on artificial intelligence (Artificial Intelligence Act) and amending certain Union legislative acts', 2021/0106(COD), 25 November. Available at: https://eur-lex.europa.eu/legal-content/EN/TXT/PDF/?uri=CONSIL:ST_15698_2022_INIT

Davis, J.P. (2018) 'Law without mind: AI, ethics, and jurisprudence', *California Western Law Review*, 55(1), p. 165.

de Matos Pinto, I. (2021) 'The draft AI Act: A success story of strengthening Parliament's right of legislative initiative?', *ERA Forum*, 22, pp. 619–641. https://doi.org/10.1007/s12027-021-00691-5

Dupré, C. (2016) 'The age of dignity human rights and constitutionalism in Europe in De Gregorio, G. (2021) 'The rise of digital constitutionalism in the European Union', *International Journal of Constitutional Law*, 19(1), p. 70. Available at: https://academic.oup.com/yel/article-abstract/35/1/715/2525281

Easterbrook, F.H. (1996) 'Cyberspace and the law of the horse', *University of Chicago Legal Forum*, 207.

European business leaders, startup founders, and investors (2023) 'European business leaders, startup founders, and investors call for regulating AI foundation models under the EU AI Act'. Available at: https://www.ai-statement.com/?utm_source=substack&utm_medium=email

European Commission (2017) 'Communication from the commission to the European parliament, the council, the european economic and social committee and the committee of the regions on the mid-term review on the implementation of the digital single market strategy: A connected digital single market for all', COM(2017) 228 final. Available at: https://eur-lex.europa.eu/legal-content/EN/TXT/?uri=COM:2017:228:FIN [Accessed: 28 December 2023]

European Commission (2018a) 'Artificial intelligence: Commission outlines a European approach to boost investment and set ethical guidelines', 25 April. Available at: https://single-market-economy.ec.europa.eu/news/commission-outlines-european-approach-artificial-intelligence-2018-04-25_en

European Commission (2018b) 'Communication from the commission to the european parliament, the European council, the council, the european economic and social committee and the committee of the regions. artificial intelligence for Europe', COM/2018/237 final. Available at: https://eur-lex.europa.eu/legal-content/EN/TXT/?uri=COM:2018:237:FIN [Accessed: 28 December 2023]

European Commission (2018c) 'Communication from the commission to the European parliament, the european council, the council, the european economic and social committee and the committee of the regions: coordinated plan on artificial intelligence', COM(2018) 795 final. Available at: https://eur-lex.europa.eu/legal-content/EN/TXT/?uri=CELEX:52018DC0795 [Accessed: 28 December 2023]

European Commission (2020a) 'White paper on artificial intelligence: A European approach to excellence and trust', 19 February. Available at: https://commission.europa.eu/publications/white-paper-artificial-intelligence-european-approach-excellence-and-trust_en [Accessed: 28 December 2023]

European Commission (2020b) 'Communication from the commission to the european parliament, the council, the European economic and social committee and the committee of the regions: A European strategy for data', COM(2020) 66 final. Available at: https://eur-lex.europa.eu/legal-content/EN/TXT/?uri=CELEX%3A52020DC0066 [Accessed: 28 December 2023]

European Commission (2020c) 'Report from the commission to the European parliament, the council and the european economic and social committee: Report on the safety and liability implications of artificial intelligence, the internet of things and robotics', COM(2020) 64 final. Available at: https://commission.europa.eu/publications/commission-report-safety-and-liability-implications-ai-internet-things-and-robotics-0_en [Accessed: 28 December 2023]

European Commission (2020d) 'Inception impact assessment on proposal for a legal act of the European parliament and the council laying down requirements for artificial intelligence', 23 July. Available at: https://ec.europa.eu/info/law/better-regulation/have-your-say/initiatives/12527-Artificial-intelligence-ethical-and-legal-requirements_en [Accessed: 28 December 2023]

European Commission (2021a) 'Proposal for a regulation of the European parliament and of the council laying down harmonised rules on artificial intelligence (artificial intelligence act) and amending certain union legislative acts', COM/2021/206 final. Available at: https://eur-lex.europa.eu/legal-content/EN/ALL/?uri=CELEX:52021PC0206 [Accessed: 26 July 2023]

European Commission (2021b) 'Communication from the commission to the European parliament, the council, the European economic and social committee and the committee of the regions: 2030 digital compass: the european way for the digital decade', COM(2021) 118 final. Available at: https://commission.europa.eu/system/files/2023-01/cellar_12e835e2-81af-11eb-9ac9-01aa75ed71a1.0001.02_DOC_1.pdf

European Commission (2022) 'Proposal for a Directive of the European Parliament and of the Councilon adapting non-contractual civil liability rules to artificial intelligence(AI Liability Directive)', COM(2022) 496 final, 28 September. Available at: https://eur-lex.europa.eu/legal-content/EN/TXT/?uri=CELEX%3A52022PC0496

European Economic and Social Committee (2017) 'Artificial Intelligence - The consequences of artificial intelligence on the (digital) single market, production, consumption, employment and society (own-initiative opinion)', INT/806-EESC-2016-01-01-05369-00-00-AC-TRA, 31 May. Available at: https://www.eesc.europa.eu/en/our-work/opinions-information-reports/opinions/artificial-intelligence-consequences-artificial-intelligence-digital-single-market-production-consumption-employment-and [Accessed: 28 December 2023]

European Parliament (2017) 'Resolution of 16 February 2017 with recommendations to the commission on civil law rules on robotics', 2015/2103(INL)

European Parliament (2020a) 'Resolution of 20 October 2020 with recommendations to the commission on a framework of ethical aspects of artificial intelligence, robotics and related technologies', 2020/2012(INL)

European Parliament (2020b) 'Resolution of 20 October 2020 with recommendations to the commission on a civil liability regime for artificial intelligence', 2020/2014(INL)

European Parliament (2020c) 'Resolution of 20 October 2020 on intellectual property rights for the development of artificial intelligence technologies', 2020/2015(INI)

European Parliament (2021b) 'Report on artificial intelligence in education, culture and the audiovisual sector', Committee on Culture and Education 2020/2017(INI), 19 April. Available at: https://www.europarl.europa.eu/doceo/document/A-9-2021-0127_EN.html [Accessed: 31 December 2023]

European Parliament (2021a) 'Report on artificial intelligence in criminal law and its use by the police and judicial authorities in criminal matters', Committee on Civil Liberties, Justice and Home Affairs, 2020/2016(INI), 13 July. Available at: https://www.europarl.europa.eu/doceo/document/A-9-2021-0232_EN.html [Accessed: 31 December 2023]

European Parliament (2023) 'Amendments adopted by the European Parliament on 14 June 2023 on the proposal for a regulation of the European Parliament and of the Council on laying down harmonised rules on artificial intelligence (Artificial Intelligence Act) and amending certain Union legislative acts', COM(2021)0206 – C9-0146/2021 – 2021/0106(COD). Available at: https://www.europarl.europa.eu/doceo/document/TA-9-2023-0236_EN.html [Accessed: 28 December 2023]

European Union Member States (2018) 'Declaration of cooperation on artificial intelligence', 10 April. Available at: https://digital-strategy.ec.europa.eu/en/news/eu-member-states-sign-cooperate-artificial-intelligence [Accessed: 28 December 2023]

Evas, T., et al. (2020a) 'Civil liability regime for artificial intelligence – European added value assessment', Directorate-General for Parliamentary Investigations, European Parliament, September. https://data.europa.eu/doi/10.2861/737677

Evas, T., et al. (2020b) 'European framework on ethical aspects of artificial intelligence, robotics and related technologies – European added value assessment', Directorate-General for Parliamentary Research Services, European Parliament. Available at: https://data.europa.eu/doi/10.2861/94107

Floridi, L. (2020) 'The fight for digital sovereignty: What it is, and why it matters, especially for the EU', *Philosophy & Technology*, 33, pp. 369–378. https://doi.org/10.1007/s13347-020-00423-6

Floridi, L. (2021) 'The European legislation on AI: A brief analysis of its philosophical approach', *Philosophy & Technology*, 34, pp. 215–222. https://doi.org/10.1007/s13347-021-00460-9

Fomin, V.V. (2018a) 'AI in the context of regulation of smart technology services', ATEITIS workshop presentation at Vytautas Magnus University, Kaunas, Lithuania, 21 September 2018.

Fuster, G.G. (2020) 'Artificial intelligence and law enforcement – impact on fundamental rights', Policy Department for Citizens' Rights and Constitutional Affairs, European Parliament, July. https://doi.org/10.2861/880024

Future of Life Institute (2021) 'FLI position on the proposal for a regulation laying down harmonised rules on artificial intelligence (Artificial Intelligence Act)', 4 August. Available at: https://futureoflife.org/wp-content/uploads/2021/08/FLI-Position-Paper-on-the-EU-AI-Act.pdf?x72900

Future Society (2021) 'Proposal for a regulation – "Artificial intelligence – Ethical and legal requirements"', *Trust in Excellence & Excellence in Trust*, August. Available at: https://thefuturesociety.org/wp-content/uploads/2021/12/The-Future-Society-response-to-AI-Act-consultation.pdf

General Secretariat of the Council (2017) 'European council meeting (19 October 2017) – Conclusions', EUCO 14/17, CO EUR 17, CONCL 5. *European Council*,

p. 7. Available at: https://www.consilium.europa.eu/media/21620/19-euco-final-conclusions-en.pdf [Accessed: 28 December 2023]

Guihot, M., et al. (2017) 'Nudging robots: Innovative solutions to regulate artificial intelligence', *Vanderbilt Journal of Entertainment and Technology Law*, 20(2), p. 385.

Hacker, P. (2023) 'The European AI liability directives – Critique of a half-hearted approach and lessons for the future', *Computer Law & Security Review*, 51, p. 105871. https://doi.org/10.1016/j.clsr.2023.105871

Hagendorff, T. (2020) 'The ethics of AI ethics: An evaluation of guidelines', *Minds & Machines*, 30, pp. 99–120. https://doi.org/10.1007/s11023-020-09517-8

High-Level Expert Group on Artificial Intelligence (2020a) 'Assessment list for trustworthy Artificial Intelligence (ALTAI) for self-assessment', 17 July. Available at: https://digital-strategy.ec.europa.eu/en/library/assessment-list-trustworthy-artificial-intelligence-altai-self-assessment [Accessed: 28 December 2023]

High-Level Expert Group on Artificial Intelligence (2020b) 'Sectoral considerations on the policy and investment recommendations for trustworthy artificial intelligence', 23 July. Available at:. Available at: https://data.europa.eu/doi/10.2759/733662 [Accessed: 28 December 2023]

High-Level Expert Group on Artificial Intelligence (HLEG AI, 2019a) 'Ethics guidelines for trustworthy AI', *European Commission*, 8 April. Available at: https://ec.europa.eu/digital-single-market/en/news/ethics-guidelines-trustworthy-ai [Accessed: 28 December 2023]

High-Level Expert Group on Artificial Intelligence (HLEG AI, 2019b) 'Policy and investment recommendations for trustworthy artificial intelligence', 26 June. Available at: https://digital-strategy.ec.europa.eu/en/library/policy-and-investment-recommendations-trustworthy-artificial-intelligence [Accessed: 28 December 2023]

Lomas, N. (2023) 'EU lawmakers eye tiered approach to regulating generative AI', *TechCrunch*, 21 April. Available at: https://tcrn.ch/3LkPkKc [Accessed: 26 July 2023]

Maas, M.M. (2021) 'Artificial intelligence governance under change: Foundations, facets, frameworks', Dissertation. University of Copenhagen.

Novelli, C. et al. (2024) Taking AI risks seriously: a new assessment model for the AI Act. *AI & Soc* 39, 2493–2497. https://doi.org/10.1007/s00146-023-01723-z

Novelli, C. (2023) 'Legal personhood for the integration of AI systems in the social context: A study hypothesis', *AI & Society*, 38, pp. 1347–1359. https://doi.org/10.1007/s00146-021-01384-w

Perarnaud, C., et al. (2022) '"Splinternets": Addressing the renewed debate on internet fragmentation', Directorate-General for Parliamentary Research Services, European Parliament. Available at: https://www.europarl.europa.eu/RegData/etudes/STUD/2022/729530/EPRS_STU(2022)729530_EN.pdf

Rossi, F. (2016) 'Artificial intelligence: Potential benefits and ethical considerations', *European Parliament Think Tank*, Briefing, 12 October. Available at: https://www.europarl.europa.eu/RegData/etudes/BRIE/2016/571380/IPOL_BRI(2016)571380_EN.pdf

Sartor, G. and Lagioia, F. (2020) 'The impact of the general data protection regulation on artificial intelligence', Directorate-General for Parliamentary Research Services, European Parliament, July. https://data.europa.eu/doi/10.2861/293

Smuha, N., et al. (2021) 'How the EU can achieve legally trustworthy AI: A response to the European commission's proposal for an artificial intelligence act', *SSRN Electronic Journal*. https://doi.org/10.2139/ssrn.3899991

Veale, M. and Borgesius, Z.F. (2021) 'Demystifying the draft EU artificial intelligence act — analysing the good, the bad, and the unclear elements of the proposed approach', *Computer Law Review International*, 22(4), pp. 97–112. https://doi.org/10.9785/cri-2021-220402

Wagner, G. (2023). 'Liability rules for the digital age — Aiming for the brussels effect', 8 January. Available at: https://ssrn.com/abstract=4320285 or http://dx.doi.org/10.2139/ssrn.4320285

Wansley, M.T. (2016) 'Regulation of emerging risks', *Vanderbilt Law Review*, 69, p. 401. Available at: https://scholarship.law.vanderbilt.edu/vlr/vol69/iss2/3

5 "The Horse" of Artificial General Intelligence Law

For the purposes of this book, Artificial General Intelligence (AGI) is defined as a *greater-than-human intelligence, which can successfully perform any intellectual task a human being can, adapt to the external environment, and even achieve self-awareness.*[1] Taxonomically, the AGI model aligns with the definition of a "general-purpose AI model", provided in Article 3 (63) of the AI Act, as a model that displays significant generality and is capable of competently performing a wide range of distinct tasks, and which can be integrated into many downstream systems or applications.

The Regulation Recitals (99) identifies large generative Artificial Intelligence (AI) models as archetypal general-purpose AI models, given that they allow for flexible generation of content, such as in the form of text, audio, images, or video, that can readily accommodate a wide range of distinctive tasks. As clarified in Recitals (97) and (100), to become a functional general-purpose AI system, a general-purpose AI model requires the addition of integration components, such as a user interface or integration into an AI system. Consequently, a general-purpose AI model can be used directly or integrated into other AI systems, including high-risk AI systems.

Where a general-purpose AI system qualifies as high-risk, comprehensive requirements are set to enforce the trustworthiness of AI systems throughout their life cycle. This includes requirements on the quality of data sets used, technical documentation, and record-keeping, transparency, the provision of information to deployers, human oversight, robustness, accuracy, and cybersecurity (Recital (66)). The provider must establish a sound quality management system, ensure the accomplishment of the required conformity assessment procedure, establish a robust post-market monitoring system (Recital (81)), and comply with other statutory obligations.

A risk management system should be established, implemented, documented, and maintained in relation to high-risk AI systems under the requirements of Article 9 of the AI Act. This system operates as a *continuous iterative*

1 Huang (2017), p. 520.

DOI: 10.4324/9781003650140-6

process planned and run throughout the entire lifecycle of a high-risk AI system, requiring regular, systematic review and updating. This should comprise several stages, including risk identification, estimation, and evaluation, and adoption of appropriate and targeted risk management measures. Operational guidance for such risk management may be derived from the standards, as overviewed and compared, for example, by Eckmaier et al.[2]

Parallel to risk management is cybersecurity, whose asset taxonomies and threat landscapes are thoroughly presented by the ENISA report on AI Cybersecurity Challenges.[3] Within the context of the AI Act, the standardisation request for cybersecurity in high-risk AI systems was addressed to European Committee for Standardization and European Committee for Electrotechnical Standardization (CEN-CENELEC), with a requirement to consult European Telecommunications Standards Institute (ETSI).[4]

Compliance obligations extend throughout the entire life cycle of high-risk AI systems. Prior to market entry, these AI systems are mandated to undergo a conformity assessment procedure to ensure their compliance with the prescribed regulatory requirements. A "CE" marking, as a visible sign of this conformity with EU regulation, is to be affixed to high-risk AI systems. Furthermore, providers are obliged to demonstrate this conformity when requested by a national competent authority. This includes a written or electronically signed EU declaration of conformity for each AI system. The declaration affirms that the high-risk AI system meets the specified requirements and must be kept at the disposal of national competent authorities for ten years post-market.

Additionally, Article 72 underlines the necessity of a robust post-market monitoring system. Providers are required to establish and document such a system, with the aim of evaluating the compliance of AI systems throughout their life cycle, as explained by Recitals (155). This system is also key to ensuring that the possible risks emerging from AI systems, which continue to "learn" after being placed on the market or put into service, can be more efficiently and timely addressed. In this context, providers must have a system in place to report any serious incidents resulting from the use of their AI systems to the relevant authorities.

The Act introduces an additional "systemic" risk class specifically applicable to general-purpose AI models. Under Article 3 (65) "systemic risk" is tied to a model's high-impact capabilities and its scale of propagation across the value chain, with foreseeable negative effects on public health, safety, public security, fundamental rights, or society as a whole. Examples of systemic risks provided by the AI Act in Recitals (110) within this context include

2 Eckmaier et al. (2022).

3 Malatras et al. (2022).

4 Junklewitz et al. (2023).

inter alia large-scale harms to safety and critical sectors, harms to democratic processes and security, and the amplification of illegal, false, or discriminatory content.

Classification of general-purpose AI models as presenting systemic risks will initially depend on computation capability, either based on a quantitative threshold of the cumulative amount of compute used for its training measured in floating point operations (FLOPs) or on an individual designation decision of the Commission considering criteria in Annex XIII (e.g., the number of parameters, quality and size of the dataset, input and output modalities, or the reach measures in business users). The initial FLOP threshold for this has been set as 10^{25} (Article 51 (2)). However, the Commission is obliged to adapt the threshold in the light of evolving technological developments, such as algorithmic improvements or increased hardware efficiency, to keep up with the state of the art, reflecting the capabilities recorded in the most advanced general-purpose AI models.

Assuming a Singularity scenario and AGI, as defined herein, it is evident that AGI architectures exceed these thresholds, representing the most sophisticated, autonomous, and responsible machine, which may pose systemic risks, as described by the AI Act. Therefore, the following observations are limited to the overview of the *lex specialis* of general-purpose AI models with systemic risks. In particular, as stated in Recitals (110), attention should be devoted to risks from alignment failures; chemical, biological, radiological, and nuclear enablement through lowered barriers; offensive cyber enablement (discovery, exploitation, operational use); use that affects physical systems and critical infrastructure; replication and automated model-training pipelines; bias and discrimination at scale; disinformation and privacy erosion with democratic spillovers; and cascade events producing city or sector level disruption.

Under this proposal (Article 53 (1)), all general-purpose AI models require keeping up-to-date technical documentation, including their training and testing process and the results of their evaluation, as information and documentation to providers of AI systems who intend to integrate the general-purpose AI model in their AI system, although "without prejudice to the need to respect and protect intellectual property rights and confidential business information or trade secrets in accordance with Union and national law".

Providers of general-purpose AI models with systemic risks, without any exceptions available under Article 53, shall also put in place a policy to comply with Union copyright law and draw up and make publicly available a sufficiently detailed summary of the content used for training of the general-purpose AI model, according to a template provided by the AI Office. Moreover, under Article 55, general-purpose AI providers with systemic risks must, in addition, perform model evaluation in accordance with standardised protocols and tools reflecting the state of the art; assess and mitigate possible systemic risks at the Union level, including their sources; monitor and report serious incidents, adopt corrective measures, and ensure an adequate level of cybersecurity protection for the model and its physical infrastructure.[5]

To prove compliance, providers of general-purpose AI models with systemic risk may rely on codes of practice within the meaning of Article 56 until a harmonised standard is published. The Commission may decide to approve a code of practice and give it general validity within the Union or to provide common rules for the implementation of the relevant obligations. Once a harmonised standard is published and assessed as suitable to cover the relevant obligations by the AI Office, compliance with a European harmonised standard should grant providers the presumption of conformity (Recital (117)). Providers of general-purpose AI models with systemic risks who do not adhere to an approved code of practice shall demonstrate alternative adequate means of compliance for approval of the Commission.

European legislators have constructed an impressive blueprint of AI regulation, despite the last-minute inclusion of concepts like systemic risks and general-purpose AI models. However, structural inadequacies remain regarding liability, privacy, intellectual property, and cybersecurity issues caused by generative AI alone.[6] When viewed through the context of the Singularity scenario, it makes it questionable whether the AI act is sufficient to regulate the unique challenges of AGI.

Critically, the AI Act emphasises that the nature of an AI system should be determined by its "intended purpose". However, this doctrine collapses when applied to AGI, a system capable of self-improvement and reprogramming itself beyond its intended purpose. Moreover, the requirement of effective human supervision, even when paired with state supervision mechanisms, becomes fragile due to the high complexity of AGI. Existing legislation or risk management systems may not adequately identify or assess risk scenarios in cases where the complexity of AGI exceeds the limits of human understanding or control, especially given the issues of jurisdictional fragmentation.

Furthermore, data governance requirements may not be relevant to AGI. The apparent ability of these systems to evolve independently of the initial training may reduce the reliability of the data sets used for that training and, thus, the effectiveness of these data management policies and best practices. Further, the potential for misuse of the power of AGI, coupled with financial motivation, surpasses any other instances of opportunistic behaviour simply because of the sheer power of AGI. Equally concerning is the absence of established anti-misuse provisions, such as integrated directives, fail-safe mechanisms, or quantified guidelines for ethical use.

Finally, AGI may present complexity levels that exceed regulatory capacity, leading to uninformed or ill-informed decisions. The risk of such

5 Kutterer (2024).
6 Novelli et al. (2024).

information asymmetry may be exacerbated by trade secrecy rules, which protect confidential business information. On the one hand, these rules are reasonable economic safeguards to prevent full disclosure of the AI model, thereby rendering research and development efforts worthless, which, in turn, would diminish the private incentive to invest and innovate.[7] On the other hand, this rule also suggests the inherent risks of opportunistic or otherwise detrimental agendas concealed behind the secrecy veil, the piercing of which may take considerable time and effort.

In sum, while the AI Act provides "The Horse", sufficient for a functional regulatory baseline, the prospects of the Singularity scenario require the "Prancing Stallion": a more agile legal framework, capable of racing against the risks that may emerge with the deployment of AGI, hopefully, sooner than a decade after the start of the race.

References

Eckmaier, R., et al. (2022) *Risk Management Standards – Analysis of Standardisation Requirements in Support of Cybersecurity Policy*. European Union Agency for Cybersecurity. https://data.europa.eu/doi/10.2824/001991

Hoeren, T. and Niehoff, M. (2018) 'Artificial intelligence in medical diagnoses and the right to explanation', *European Data Protection Law Review*, 4(3), pp. 308–319. https://doi.org/10.21552/edpl/2018/3/9

Huang, T.J. (2017) Imitating the brain with neurocomputer a "new" way towards artificial general intelligence. *International Journal of Automation and Computing*, 14(5), pp. 520–531. https://doi.org/10.1007/s11633-017-1082-y

Junklewitz, H., et al. (2023) 'Cybersecurity of artificial intelligence in the AI act', Publications Office of the European Union, Luxembourg. https://doi.org/10.2760/271009, JRC134461

Kutterer, C. (2024) 'Regulating foundation models in the AI Act: From "High" to "Systemic" Risk', [online] *MIAI – ai-regulation.com*. Available at: https://ai-regulation.com/regulating-foundation-models-in-the-ai-act-from-high-to-systemic-risk/?utm_source=substack&utm_medium=email#_ftnref17 [Accessed: 23 January 2024]

Malatras, A. and Dede, G. (eds.) (2022) *AI Cybersecurity Challenges — Threat Landscape for Artificial Intelligence*. European Union Agency for Cybersecurity. https://data.europa.eu/doi/10.2824/238222

Novelli, C., et al. (2024) 'Generative AI in EU law: Liability, privacy, intellectual property, and cybersecurity'. Available at: https://ssrn.com/abstract=4694565 or http://dx.doi.org/10.2139/ssrn.4694565

7 Hoeren and Niehoff (2018).

6 Aren't We "Missing-Something"?

Recitals (G) of the Civil Law Rules on Robotics[1] acknowledged that in the long term, the trend leans towards developing smart and autonomous machines with the capacity to be trained and make decisions independently. Within this context, the European Parliament[2] has called on the European Commission to explore all possible legal solutions, including the creation of:

> a specific legal status of electronic persons for the most sophisticated autonomous robots, responsible for making good any damage they may cause, and possibly applying electronic personality to cases where robots make autonomous decisions or otherwise interact with third parties independently.

The "most sophisticated machines", qualifying for electronic personality herein, are defined by two key properties: autonomy and responsibility. The former is understood as purely technological, while the latter is a matter of legal architecture.

Technically, the European Parliament defined machine autonomy as "the ability to take decisions and implement them in the outside world, independently of external control or influence".[3] That is, the concept of autonomy lies in the behavioural characteristics of the machine, which allows at least some room for unsupervised decision-making. If this is the case, the machine is not entirely under the control of human actors – particularly in accident situations. This feature distinguishes autonomous systems from more traditional devices that run on deterministic computer code that does not allow for machine learning or autonomous decisions. Specifying characteristics of autonomous robots, the European Parliament[4] called to take into consideration (i) the capacity to acquire autonomy through sensors and/or by exchang-

1 European Parliament (2017).
2 European Parliament (2017), Article 59 (f).
3 European Parliament, 2017), Recitals (AA).
4 European Parliament (2017), Article (1).

DOI: 10.4324/9781003650140-7

ing data with its environment (inter-connectivity); (ii) the capacity to learn through experience and interaction; (iii) at least a minor physical support; (iv) the capacity to adapt its behaviour and actions to the environment; and (v) the absence of life in the biological sense.

However, the European Parliament did not provide a doctrinal explanation or framework for the content of this new type of personhood, and it was immediately met with criticism by experts, industry leaders, and specialists from the fields of law, medicine, and ethics. In their Open Letter to the European Commission, they concluded that "creating a legal status of electronic 'person' would be ideological and nonsensical and non-pragmatic", arguing that:

> From a technical perspective based on an overvaluation of the actual capabilities of even the most advanced robots, a superficial understanding of unpredictability and self-learning capacities and, a robot perception distorted by Science-Fiction and a few recent sensational press announcements. From an ethical and legal perspective, creating a legal personality for a robot is inappropriate whatever the legal status model.[5]

Many joined this position. Floridi and Taddeo ironically noted that "Romans knew better: the owner of an enslaved person was fully responsible for any damage caused by that person". They applied this rule within the argument that attributing Electronic Personhood to robots risks misplacing moral responsibility, causal accountability, and legal liability. In their view, robots could be blamed and punished instead of humans, and irresponsible people would dismiss the need for care in the engineering, marketing, and use of robots.[6]

Bryson et al. also reviewed the utility and history of legal fiction of personhood, discussing salient precedents where such fiction resulted in abuse or incoherence. They concluded that difficulties in holding electronic persons accountable outweigh the highly precarious moral interests that AI legal personhood might protect, holding the European Parliament's legislative action "morally unnecessary and legally troublesome" and the case for Electronic Personhood fundamentally "weak" (Bryson et al., 2017).

Conversely, while the authors of the Robotics Open Letter and others argue against Electronic Legal Personhood based on current robot capabilities, Gordon suggests that their views are based on a "deficient understanding of the concept of personhood".[7] He criticises their reliance on the belief that only human beings can be persons, calling it a "highly controversial position in moral philosophy" and labelling it as speciesism and biased as well.

5 Open Letter (2018).
6 Floridi and Taddeo (2018).
7 Gordon (2020).

Gordon argues that biological characteristics like DNA should not define personhood but rather mental capabilities such as rationality, autonomy, and intelligence. Therefore, he suggests if robots could meet these criteria, denying them a legal status on the grounds that it would undermine human rights or simply because they are not human represents a misleading and biased view of the potential of non-human artificial beings.[8]

Ultimately, the regulatory consensus shifted toward the sceptics. High-Level Expert Group on AI (HLEG AI) explored the suggested legal solutions for the most sophisticated autonomous robots. In its Policy and Investment Recommendations for Trustworthy AI,[9] experts recommended refraining from establishing a legal personality for AI systems or robots. They believed this to be fundamentally inconsistent with the principle of human agency, accountability, and responsibility, and to carry the risk of a significant moral hazard. The European Commission Expert Group on Liability and New Technologies also reaffirmed the general position that for the purposes of liability, it is not necessary to give autonomous systems a legal personality.[10] These experts believed that harm caused by even fully autonomous technologies is generally reducible to risks attributable to natural persons or existing categories of legal persons. Where this is not the case, new laws directed at individuals are a better response than creating a new category of legal persons. However, experts stressed that they only looked at the liability side of things and did not take any kind of position on the future development of company law and issues such as whether an AI could act as a member of a board.[11]

Concurrently, the European Parliamentary Research Service has also published briefings and studies critical of the concept, including "What If Algorithms Could Abide by Ethical Principles?",[12] "Artificial Intelligence Ante Portas: Legal & Ethical Reflections",[13] "A Governance Framework for Algorithmic Accountability and Transparency",[14] "Should We Fear Artificial Intelligence?",[15] and "The Ethics of Artificial Intelligence: Issues and Initiatives".[16] All of these studies criticised the idea of Electronic Legal Personhood. The study of Fox-Skelly et al. rhetorically questioned, "Is it the AI itself that is responsible for its actions and consequences, or the person(s) who built them?" asserting that legal responsibility lies with the creator, consequently advocating for a ban on attributing responsibility to robots.

8 Gordon (2020).
9 HLEG AI (2020).
10 European Commission (2019).
11 European Commission (2019).
12 Kritikos (2018).
13 Kritikos (2019).
14 European Parliament (2019).
15 Brundage et al. (2018).
16 Fox-Skelly et al. (2020).

Within this critical response, the European Parliament gave up on the initial idea. In three Resolutions on the ethical and legal aspects of Artificial Intelligence software systems issued in 2020,[17] the European Parliament was adamant about not providing AI software systems with legal personality – a reversal which some consider a mistake.[18] The Civil Liability Resolution expressly stated that it is not necessary to give legal personality to AI systems since they have neither legal personality nor human conscience, and that their sole task is to serve humanity, noting that damages are nearly always the result of someone building, deploying, or interfering with the systems.[19] In the context of intellectual property rights (IPR), the IPR for AI Resolution also pointed out the negative impact of legal personality on AI technologies on incentives for human creators, holding that it would not be appropriate to seek to impart such personality.[20]

Overall, the EU regulators clearly adhere to the opinion that there are no compelling arguments for the real benefits of such personhood. Naturally, the AI Act is silent on the legal personality of AI systems, thus excluding the possibility of assigning to AI systems any status as a legal person, with rights and duties, such as the possibility of owning property, entering into contracts, suing and being sued.[21] As Floridi praised, the AI Act avoids any sci-fi speculations about AI, which "irresponsibly distracted not only the public but initially also the work of the European Parliament".[22] In his opinion, AI is a technology for solving problems and performing tasks, not some kind of Frankenstein's monster; thus, the responsibility of any AI system is entirely with the people who design, manufacture, market, and use it.

However, the European Parliament has not suggested that robots should be treated like humans in the same way as companies are, nor has it suggested using any of the established legal status models.[23] The European Parliament recognised that robot autonomy is of a "purely technological nature" and specifies a "designed to be" degree of independence from an outside human supervisor in the execution of a task in a natural environment.[24]

Indeed, current legal systems have been designed to affect only humans. They have worked well thus far since decision-making and transacting were primarily human activities, and conventional legal tools were created to assist them. However, conventional frameworks' attempts to threaten, cajole, bribe,

17 European Parliament (2020a, 2020b, 2020c).
18 Papakonstantinou and De Hert (2020).
19 European Parliament (2020b), Article 7.
20 European Parliament (2020c), Article 13.
21 Floridi and Taddeo (2018).
22 Floridi (2021).
23 Guével (2018).
24 Palmerini et al. (2014).

educate, and moralise are not applicable to non-humans.[25] So, can these legal systems, tailored to regulate "Horse" issues, cope with the challenges posed by AGI? Or must new legal categories be created with their specific features and implications?[26] This question becomes critical if AI will one day reach such a high level of development that it starts giving itself new goals and building new artefacts to reach them, all this independently of humans who may become irrelevant at best, extinct at worst.[27] Therefore, in line with Lessig's[28] commentaries, the potential of the proposed horse law to regulate the most sophisticated, autonomous, and responsible machines (such as AGI) may be overconfidently overestimated.

In conclusion, the European Parliament's decision to reject the idea of an Electronic Legal Personhood status could be prudent, taking into account the current level of AI development and the lack of arguments justifying the necessity of such legal development. However, on the other side of these "missing-something" arguments lies a grain of cognitive apathy, a lack of foresight, or simply insufficient AGI risk assessment.

References

Bostrom, N. (2014) *Superintelligence: Paths, Dangers, Strategies*. Oxford: Oxford University Press.

Brundage, M., et al. (2018) 'Should we fear artificial intelligence? – In-depth analysis', Directorate-General for Parliamentary Research Services, European Parliament. https://data.europa.eu/doi/10.2861/412165

Bryson, J.J., et al.(2017) 'Of, for, and by the people: the legal lacuna of synthetic persons',Artificial Intelligence and Law, 25, pp. 273–291. doi:10.1007/s10506-017-9214-9

European Commission (2019) 'Liability for artificial intelligence and other emerging digital technologies', Directorate-General for Justice and Consumers Publications Office. https://data.europa.eu/doi/10.2838/573689

European Parliament (2017) 'Resolution of 16 February 2017 with recommendations to the commission on civil law rules on robotics', 2015/2103(INL)

European Parliament (2019) 'A governance framework for algorithmic accountability and transparency', Directorate-General for Parliamentary Research Services Publications Office. Available at: https://data.europa.eu/doi/10.2861/59990

European Parliament (2020a) 'Resolution of 20 October 2020 with recommendations to the Commission on a framework of ethical aspects of artificial intelligence, robotics and related technologies', 2020/2012(INL)

European Parliament (2020b) 'Resolution of 20 October 2020 with recommendations to the Commission on a civil liability regime for artificial intelligence', 2020/2014(INL)

25 Viljanen (2017).

26 European Parliament (2017), Recitals (AC).

27 Bostrom (2014).

28 Lessig (1999).

European Parliament (2020c) 'Resolution of 20 October 2020 on intellectual property rights for the development of artificial intelligence technologies', 2020/2015(INI)

Floridi, L. (2021) 'The European legislation on AI: a Brief Analysis of its Philosophical Approach', *Philosophy & Technology*, 34, pp. 215–222. https://doi.org/10.1007/s13347-021-00460-9

Floridi, L. and Taddeo, M. (2018) 'Romans would have denied robots legal personhood', *Nature*, 557(7705), p. 309. https://doi.org/10.1038/d41586-018-05154-5

Fox-Skelly, J., et al. (2020) 'The ethics of artificial intelligence – issues and initiatives', Directorate-General for Parliamentary Research Services, European Parliament. Available at: https://data.europa.eu/doi/10.2861/6644

Gordon, J.S. (2020) 'What do we owe to intelligent robots?', *AI & Society*, 35, pp. 209–223. https://doi.org/10.1007/s00146-018-0844-6

Guével, C. (Interviewer) (2018) 'Mady delvaux-stehres (European Parliament): "There is no way a robot should be treated like a human being"', *Leaders League*, 19 April. Available at: https://www.leadersleague.com/en/news/mady-delvaux-stehres-european-parliament-there-is-no-way-a-robot-should-be-treated-like-a-human-being

High-Level Expert Group on Artificial Intelligence (HLEG, 2020) 'Sectoral considerations on the policy and investment recommendations for trustworthy artificial intelligence', 23 July. Available at: https://data.europa.eu/doi/10.2759/733662 [Accessed: 28 December 2023]

Kritikos, M. (2018) 'What if algorithms could abide by ethical principles?', European Parliamentary Research Service, Panel for the Future of Science and Technology (STOA), 20 November. Available at: https://www.europarl.europa.eu/thinktank/en/document/EPRS_ATA(2018)624267

Kritikos, M. (2019) 'Artificial Intelligence ante portas: Legal & ethical reflections?', European Parliamentary Research Service, Scientific Foresight Unit (STOA), PE 634.427. Available at: https://www.europarl.europa.eu/thinktank/en/document/EPRS_BRI(2019)634427

Lessig, L. (1999) 'The law of the horse: What cyberlaw might teach', *Harvard Law Review*, 113(2), pp. 501–549. https://doi.org/10.2307/1342331

Open Letter (2018) 'to the European commission artificial intelligence and robotics', *Politico*. https://www.politico.eu/wp-content/uploads/2018/04/RoboticsOpenLetter.pdf

Palmerini, E., et al. (2014) 'Guidelines on regulating robotics', Report on Regulating Emerging Robotic Technologies in Europe: Robotics Facing Law and Ethics, Collaborative Project (CP). Available at: http://www.robolaw.eu/ [Accessed: 1 May 2017]

Papakonstantinou, V. and De Hert, P. (2020) 'Refusing to award legal personality to AI: Why the European Parliament got it wrong', *European Law Blog*, 25 November. Available at: https://europeanlawblog.eu/2020/11/25/refusing-to-award-legal-personality-to-ai-why-the-european-parliament-got-it-wrong/

Viljanen, M. (2017) 'A cyborg turn in law?', *German Law Journal*, 18(5), pp. 1277–1308. https://doi.org/10.1017/s2071832200022331

7 Foundations of Neo-Institutional Analysis

The underlying belief system guiding this book rests on the economic approach to law, which has gained recognition as "the most important development in legal scholarship of the twentieth century".[1] The application of economic theories provides a valuable normative standard in predicting the effects of laws on behaviour and evaluating the efficiency of law and policy.[2] Not surprisingly, economic analysis has been applied to regulatory issues across a wide range of legal disciplines,[3] including computer science and Artificial Intelligence (AI).[4]

That said, the inquiry into a legal regulation framework for the Artificial General Intelligence (AGI) may be held to be an inquiry into "the humanly devised constraints that structure political, economic, and social interactions ... to create order and reduce uncertainty in exchange", in other words – *institutions*.[5] Under this approach, the issues of legal regulation of AGI, same as determinants of institutions, are susceptible to analysis by the tools of economic theory.[6]

The design of an institutional environment and institutions of governance are two main parts of the New Institutional Economics – one of the dominant economic theories of the twenty-first century, greatly influenced by notable figures such as Nobel Laureates Ronald Coase, Herbert Simon, Olivier E. Williamson, Douglass North, and James Buchanan.[7] This powerful school of thought offers an esteemed set of analytical tools drawn from various disciplines in the social sciences, business, and law.[8] This toolbox also includes

1 Cooter and Ulen (2016); Salzberger (2007).
2 See, e.g., Cooter (1995, 1998); Cooter and Ulen (2016); Blackwood (1996); Williamson (2000b) and others.
3 See, e.g., Posner (2014); Coase (1960); Calabresi (1970); Cooter and Ulen (2016) and others.
4 See, e.g., Peng et al. (2021); Wagner (2020); Schuster (2018); Casey and Niblett (2017); Gomes (2018) and others.
5 North (1991).
6 Williamson (2000a).
7 Obińska-Wajda (2016).
8 Alston (2008).

DOI: 10.4324/9781003650140-8

transaction cost theory,[9] which is used herein as one of the leading approaches to the researched issues.

Overall, economics' theoretical underpinnings and philosophical stance serve as a valid scientific approach to explaining the legal design of AGI regulation. Therefore, the choice of economic theories to construct a legal framework is a sound methodological approach. The next step is to structure the analytical framework and identify the levels and units of analysis. These, consequently, will serve as a taxonomy for the subsequent design of the legal regulation framework for the AGI.

7.1 Levels of Analysis

The analytical architecture relies on the four levels of social analysis, elaborated by Oliver E. Williamson[10] (see Table 7.1). In his scheme, Williamson distinguishes between four levels, each of which serves a different purpose in the workings of the economy. This institutional approach is inherently human-centric since social institutions originate from individual behaviour.[11] As such, it is in compliance with the spirit of the EU AI Act, which promotes said human-centric approach.

Table 7.1 Levels of social analysis

Level	*Frequency of change (years)*	*Purpose*
Embeddedness: informal institutions, customs, traditions, norms, religion	100 to 1000	Often noncalculative, spontaneous
Institutional environment: formal rules of the game – esp. property (polity, judiciary, bureaucracy)	10 to 100	Get the institutional environment right. 1st order economising
Governance: play of the game – esp. contract (aligning governance structures with transactions)	1 to 10	Get the governance structures right. 2nd order economising
Resource allocation and employment: prices and quantities, incentive alignment	Continuous	Get the marginal conditions right. 3rd order economising

9 For exhaustive analysis of the transaction cost theory, its elements and developments see, e.g., Ruester (2010); Macher and Richman (2008); Geyskens et al. (2006); Carter and Hodgson (2006) and others.

10 Williamson (1998, 2000a).

11 Obińska-Wajda (2016).

According to Williamson,[12] this institutional system is fully interconnected. The solid arrows connecting a higher level with a lower level signify that the higher level imposes constraints on the level immediately below. The reverse arrows connecting lower with higher levels are dashed and signal feedback. Each level has its rich subset of theories, models, and insights, as briefly observed below.

7.1.1 Level 1: Embeddedness

"The top level is the social embeddedness level. This is where the norms, customs, mores, traditions, etc. are located. Religion plays a large role at this level".[13]

This "informal order" consists of the non-law aspects of culture that compel people to behave, such as basic trust, social networks, shared myths, and narratives. As Kenneth Arrow noted, societies "in their evolution have developed implicit agreements to certain kinds of regard for others, agreements which are essential to the survival of the society or at least contribute greatly to the efficiency of its working".[14] According to Williamson,[15] institutions at this level are often unspoken and implicit, taken for granted, and change very slowly – on the order of centuries or millennia, and thus have a lasting grip on the way society conducts itself.

Many of these informal institutions have spontaneous origins and display a great deal of inertia – which is to say that deliberative choice of a calculative kind is minimally implicated.[16] When people observe some behaviour, they more or less spontaneously approve or disapprove of it (or fail to react) and then reward, penalise, or ignore the actor.[17] Notably, within this context, state-backed sanctions are not the only option when it comes to the enforcement of such customary rules and obligations. One of the central insights of the custom-and-law literature is that social sanctions, such as gossip and exclusion, can be, and often are, just as effective in ensuring compliance with customary rules.[18] Informal norms, despite their unwritten form, resemble a law, except that a neighbour sanctions the violator of a norm, whereas a judge sanctions the violator of a law.[19]

Accordingly, this layer of social analysis refers to legal norms not necessarily derived from legislation. For example, customary law is universally

12 Williamson (1998, 2000a).
13 Williamson (1998).
14 Arrow (1974).
15 Williamson (1998, 2000a).
16 Williamson (1998, 2000a).
17 Posner (1996).
18 Blocher (2012).
19 Posner (1996).

accepted as an unwritten form of international law that gains its authority not from legislation but from general practice accepted as law through common and continuous usage.[20] Also, diamond merchants and gangs are among the most famous examples who actually govern themselves through custom.[21] Here, to function, the meaning of the rule needs to be established through some degree of *trust*[22] and practical sense-making, which reveals the rule's meaning and makes regulation effective.[23]

Furthermore, within these institutions are some abstract and indefinite legislated value statements, making them ontologically non-positivistic, such as the principle of "good morals"[24] or, as in the case of Trustworthy AI – lawfulness, robustness, and other foundational ethical principles of AI. Despite their lack of specificity, these *prime directives* are (should be) a decisive factor in decision-making.

Williamson[25] contends that Level 1 is taken as given by most institutional economists, who predominantly focus on Levels 2 and 3. Be that as it may, for lawyers, this level embodies the spiritual and moral heritage that forms the foundation of indivisible, universal values such as human dignity, freedom, equality, and solidarity, enshrined in the Charter of Fundamental Rights of the European Union, and relevant international human rights law. In essence, Level 1 encapsulates the imaginative "idea of law" as the embodiment of right reason, also known as the "rule of law" (expressing what law ought to be). This higher level imposes constraints on the institutional environment level immediately below. Therefore, the idea of law is (should be) the basic *analytical model* to guide legislative decisions and set the discretionary boundaries of rule-making or rule-enforcing institutional powers.

7.1.2 Level 2: Institutional Environment

"The second level is referred to as the institutional environment … get the formal rules of the game right".[26]

The "rules of the game", defined at this level of social analysis, are the product of politics, within which economic activity is organised. The polity, judiciary, and bureaucracy of government are all located here.[27] These systems define the parameters within which economic and social activity takes

20 Vaišvila (2004); Schmitt and Vihul (2014).
21 Blocher (2012).
22 Granovetter (1985).
23 Fomin (2018).
24 Kaufmann (1963).
25 Williamson (2000a).
26 Williamson (2000a).
27 Williamson (1998).

place. For example, they determine how contracts are enforced, how property is protected, and how the political system operates.

Legal regulation at this level can be narrowly analysed through the lens of legislative intent (the "law of rules"), manifested by the government's expression of what law is. The typical form of this expression comes with the positivistic legal rules and their formal enforcement orders, either under the threat of sanctions or by offering rewards.[28] For example, seven key requirements for Trustworthy AI[29] and the following institutional arrangements qualify as belonging to this level of social analysis as an operational model aimed to implement the requirements of lawfulness, robustness, and other foundational ethical principles of Trustworthy AI.

These formal rules (constitutions, laws, property rights) are partly the product of evolutionary processes and include the executive, legislative, judicial, and bureaucratic functions of government, as well as the distribution of powers across different levels of government.[30] Williamson[31] notes that absent any massive discontent (due to wars, occupations or breakdowns, financial crises, and alike), major changes in the rules of the game occur in the order of decades or centuries.

Williamson[32] highlighted that the definition and enforcement of property rights are important at this level. Property rights are a set of rights to take permissible actions to use, transfer, or otherwise exploit or enjoy property. Williamson strongly agreed[33] with Coase's[34] argument that:

> a private-enterprise system cannot function properly unless property rights are created in resources, and, when this is done, someone wishing to use a resource has to pay the owner to obtain it. Chaos disappears, and so does the government, except that a legal system to define property rights and to arbitrate disputes is, of course, necessary.

Although these rights are sometimes enforced by Level 1 type of norms, like etiquette, social custom, and social ostracism,[35] an essential function of the

28 Vaišvila (2004); Hertog (1999).

29 Human agency and oversight; technical robustness and safety; privacy and data governance; transparency; diversity, non-discrimination, and fairness; societal and environmental well-being; accountability (HLEG AI, 2019).

30 Williamson (2000a).

31 Williamson (2000a).

32 Williamson (2000a).

33 "Once property rights have been defined and their enforcement assured, the government steps aside. Resources are allocated to their highest value as the marvel of the market works its wonders" (Williamson, 2000a).

34 Coase (1959).

35 Ménard and Shirley (2014).

institutional environment at this level is "the creation of polities that will create and enforce efficient property rights".[36]

It shall be noted here that an overly narrow (positivistic) approach to legal regulation may result in a perversion of law, as was attempted with the defence of "superior orders" at the Nuremberg Trials. The argument that one must obey even the basest statute, provided it was enacted with formal correctness, can no longer be deemed valid considering the experiences with fascist and communist dictatorships.[37] On the other hand, an excessively broad (naturalistic) appeal to the vague *ideas of law* may also lead to the same perverted result. For example, courts, invoking an alleged "spirit" of the law, may disregard valid and well-founded legislative intent that stands in the way of their desired (or demanded) decision. Ultimately, extreme positivistic or extreme naturalistic approaches are neither desirable nor tolerable.[38] Instead, the design of regulation should aim for an efficient balance that incorporates the best of both perspectives. Indeed, since both externalised "legislative will" (Level 2) and internalised "right reason" (Level 1) approaches propose forms of control, both should be considered as co-working tools to achieve the desired impact of legal regulation.

Ideally, when confronted with emerging behaviours, regulators (legislative, executive, and/or judicial branches of government) should foreplay scrutinising *what law ought to be* according to the "idea of law" (Level 1) and intercourse with the conversion of *what law is* according to the "law of rules" (Level 2) within these new contexts of legal relationships. This way, institutions at both levels evolve as novel contexts are introduced for regulatory considerations. Presumably, this dynamic system constantly adjusts toward a constitutional equilibrium[39] where, within the confines of the *rule of law*, legal omissions are filled with the *law of rules* and the desired behaviour is internalised by the subjects to this regulation. However, since the internalisation of rules is not that straightforward, society needs systems for the arbitration of disputes and enforcement of rights and obligations, as already mentioned – either under the threat of sanctions or by offering rewards.

7.1.3 Level 3: Governance

"The third level, which is where the institutions of governance are located … get the governance structures right".[40]

36 North (1994); Williamson (2000a).

37 Kaufmann (1963).

38 Kaufmann (1963).

39 It is the ideal condition produced by the application of the norms of constitutional law in a given legal order, involving two aspects, which reflect the basic functions of constitutional law: (i) the protection of fundamental rights and (ii) the balancing of powers (Celeste, 2019).

40 Williamson (2000a).

This level goes beyond the "rules of the game" (property) to include the "play of the game" (contract) in social analysis. It deals with the ways in which economic activity is organised within the framework defined by Levels 1 and 2. According to Williamson,[41] the need for a legal system for defining contract laws and enforcing contracts is posed herein.

Within this context, the definition of contract typically involves a debtor's manifestation of intention (promise) to act or refrain from acting in a specific way vis-à-vis another or others (creditors), which the law in some way recognises as an enforceable obligation, providing a remedy to creditors in case of a breach. That is, a singular contract is based on the concept of promise-with-law.[42] Notably, in a society where all promises are kept as intended, the contract laws and enforcing institutions are stealthy (at least) or irrelevant (at most). However, some of the promises made today will be breached tomorrow. Therefore, the principle of *pacta sunt servanda* (agreements must be kept), although foundational in theory, is utopian in reality. Accordingly, to diminish the risks of breach, pre-contractual legal institutions (such as good faith and fair dealing obligations) are needed, but if *ex ante* institutions fail, parties to a contract are forced towards the *ex post* process of enforcement through private or state ordering institutions. This "play of the game" forms the content of this level of social analysis.

That is, according to Williamson,[43] at this level, the governance of contractual relations is the focus of analysis, where governance is understood as an effort to craft *order*, thereby mitigating conflict and realising *mutual gains*. It includes the structure of firms, the nature of contractual relationships, and the systems of governance that manage these relationships. Williamson[44] noted that possible reorganisation of transactions among governance structures is re-examined periodically, on the order of a year to a decade, often as a response to economic conditions or contract renewal intervals.

Williamson noted that costless court ordering being a fiction, much of the conflict settlement action is dealt with directly by the parties.[45] Therefore, private ordering of sanctions or rewards is also settled at this level of social analysis. This might involve technical and non-technical methods to "play the game" in compliance with the principles and rules formed at higher levels. For instance, automated clause execution tools whose transparency and immutability replace the trust between parties, so-called "smart contracts", have garnered significant interest from market analysts, academia, the media,

41 Williamson (2000a).
42 Macneil (1974, p. 693).
43 Williamson (2000a).
44 Williamson (2000a).
45 Williamson (2000a).

and the public at large.[46] Indeed, the rapid and exponential growth of data, computation, and storage capacity has led to the rise of LegalTech, RegTech, GovTech, and other innovations, disrupting the ways in which economic activity is organised.

7.1.4 Level 4: Resource Allocation and Employment

"The fourth level … is the level at which neoclassical analysis works. Optimality apparatus, often marginal analysis, is employed, and the firm, for these purposes, is typically described as a production function".[47]

This is the most immediate level of social analysis, dealing with the day-to-day decisions of individuals and firms. This is where the data on events, artefacts, and contextual knowledge is born. It includes the individual choices about work, consumption, saving, or investment, and the corporate choices about production and pricing. These decisions are typically modelled in traditional economic analysis using concepts like supply and demand, marginal cost, and marginal benefit. Changes at this level are continuous and reflect the ongoing process of economic decision-making. Williamson[48] notes that adjustments to prices and output occur more or less continuously.

It shall be noted here that for some day-to-day resource allocation and employment transactions, costs are low because informal norms (embeddedness) suffice to uphold bargains. Most local communities have well-established customs that limit opportunistic behaviour. Similarly, repeated transactions often give a sufficient incentive to deal fairly. However, though local or repeated exchanges may have low transaction costs, the gains from such trade are limited because the extent of the market limits the number of individuals with whom one can deal locally or repeatedly. Formal institutions and governance, including access to justice, are necessary to safeguard market participants engaged in anonymous or non-simultaneous exchanges if the full gains in an extended market are to be captured. In the absence of an institutional environment and governance, including honest courts, resource allocation and employment transaction costs will be higher.[49]

Overall, this four-tier social analysis framework offers a holistic view of the workings of the economy and, therefore, may serve as a taxonomy for AGI risk analysis and the subsequent design of the legal regulation framework. Such an approach ensures consideration of the complex relations between social, economic, and legal dimensions in the design of the

46 European Securities and Markets Authority (2020).
47 Williamson (2000a).
48 Williamson (2000a).
49 Alston (2008).

regulatory environment, which must respond to the challenges posed by AGI technologies to any or all of these levels of social analysis.

7.2 Unit of Analysis

The atomic unit of this framework is the *transaction*, the foundational unit of analysis in the Williamson framework.[50] A transaction occurs when a good or service is transferred across a technologically separable interface – one stage of activity terminates, and another begins.[51] So defined, a transaction can be decomposed into four constitutive elements: (i) the activity (i.e., a well-defined step in the transfer process), (ii) the case (i.e., a transfer process instance), (iii) the performer, also referred to as the originator (i.e., the person or system executing or initiating the activity), and (iv) the time context (i.e., each transaction has a timestamp and may be totally ordered).

Accordingly, transactions can be analysed from at least three perspectives, systematised by Günther:[52]

(1) *The Case Perspective* answers the "*What?*" question by focusing on the properties and path of the specific case;
(2) *The Originator Perspective* answers the "*Who?*" question by mapping the originator field and the relationships between performers;
(3) *The Process Perspective* answers the "*How?*" question by analysing the control flow and ordering of activities.

These perspectives help to isolate the concrete situations that justify legal intervention, identifying who originates and owns the transaction, and how we should order the activities for the most efficient outcomes. This trifecta forms a complete view of the legal regulation framework for any phenomenon, including AGI.

At the core of the economic analysis is the assumption that every transaction comes at a certain cost due to the necessities of search, negotiation, and control. According to Coase,[53] these are "sufficiently costly at any rate to prevent many transactions that would be carried out in a world in which the pricing system worked without cost". Transaction costs, although with an enormous amount of theoretical and empirical controversy,[54] are proclaimed

50 Williamson (1998, 2000a, 2000b).
51 Williamson (1975, 1996); Posner (2004).
52 Günther (2009).
53 Coase (1960).
54 Medema and Zerbe (2000).

to be the "costs of running the economic system",[55] constituting the central economic efficiency problem.[56]

Assuming that efficiency and justice coincide in many ways,[57] transaction costs are a prime legal concern, too. Williamson[58] compared transaction costs with frictions in mechanical systems, noting that:

> with a well-working interface, as with a well-working machine, these transfers occur smoothly. In mechanical systems we look for frictions: do the gears mesh, are the parts lubricated, is there needless slippage or other loss of energy? The economic counterpart of friction is transaction cost: for that subset of transactions where it is important to elicit cooperation, do the parties to the exchange operate harmoniously, or are there frequent misunderstandings and conflicts that lead to delays, breakdowns, and other malfunctions?

According to Williamson,[59] these misunderstandings and conflicts are mediated by governance structures (markets, hybrids, hierarchies). The "genius of neoclassical economics"[60] is that there are large numbers of transactions where conscious cooperation between traders is not necessary. The invisible hand works well if each party can go its way with little cost to the other. Transaction cost economics is concerned with the "frictions" of market failures and the hazards that come with them.[61]

The famous version of the market failure problem is an illustrative proposition known as the Coase Theorem.[62] The general claim here is that if transactions are costless, their outcome is efficient regardless of the legal regulation. That is, the enforcement of rights or obligations is irrelevant, and all transactions are complete. However, since the possibility of zero transaction costs was "a very unrealistic assumption",[63] the real message was to study the world with positive transaction costs.[64]

55 Arrow (1969).
56 Marinescu (2012); Williamson and Tadelis (2012).
57 Šimašius (2002).
58 Williamson (1996).
59 Williamson (1996).
60 Williamson (1996).
61 Ruester (2010); Gomes (2018); Williamson (1971, 1996).
62 By using an example of crop damage caused by straying cattle, Coase (1960) proposed the following: "it is necessary to know whether the damaging business is liable or not for damage caused since without the establishment of this initial delimitation of rights there can be no marked transactions to transfer and recombine them. But the ultimate result (which maximizes the value of production) is independent of the legal position if the pricing system is assumed to work without cost".
63 Coase (1960).
64 Williamson and Tadelis (2012).

Accordingly, the analytical challenge within this line of thought is to identify, evaluate, and respond to the reasons why these "frictions" of economic systems (market failures) appear in the first place and, consequently, what governance institutions we should apply (i.e., how we will "play the game") and within what institutional environment (i.e., what are the "rules of the game"), so that the allocation of resources and labour would be efficient. That is, we need to understand the nature and sources of these potential transaction costs and how they can be prevented.[65]

The market failure factors that cause transaction costs and consequently determine social institutions can be broadly categorised into four groups (Williamson, 1986):

1) *Bounded rationality*, which recognises that humans are "intendedly rational, but only limited so".[66] *Bounded rationality* involves limited cognitive competencies (impossibility of receiving, storing, retrieving, and processing all information without any error) and language limits (inability to articulate knowledge and information clearly to be perfectly understood by others, i.e., miscommunication and misinterpretation).[67] Within this context, de Backer[68] identified a total of 151 cognitive biases, i.e., irrational "errors" that are programmed into people's brains and affect the decision-making process;
2) *Opportunism*, which describes the self-interested nature of people who sometimes make strategic decisions in a way to achieve an individual advantage by bad faith or irresponsible behaviour. That is, sometimes humans either lack dedication in performing to the best of their competencies or seek self-interest with guile;[69]
3) *Uncertainty*, which describes the future state of nature, price and demand levels, innovations, legal and behavioural instabilities, and many other characteristics that make it impossible to predict the outcome of one's promises.[70] *Uncertainty* and *bounded rationality* are sometimes characterised as informational and cognitive inability;[71]
4) *Asset specificity*, which is a specialised investment that cannot be redeployed to alternative uses or by alternative users except at a loss of productive value.[72] It usually describes six types of specific assets that create bilateral dependency on the scarce resources and identity of the

65 Acemoğlu (2022).
66 Simon (1976).
67 Ruester (2010); Williamson (1986); Simon (1976).
68 de Backer (2026).
69 Ruester (2010); Williamson (1986).
70 Williamson (1991).
71 Nobre (2011).
72 Williamson (1996).

> transacting actor. These are (i) site specificity, (ii) physical asset specificity, (iii) dedicated assets, (iv) human asset specificity, (v) intangible assets, and (vi) temporal specificity.[73]

In combination, *bounded rationality* and *uncertainty* make it impossible to evaluate all the risks related to relevant transactions and safeguards at the *ex ante* transactional stage. Consequently, all transactions have gaps and are incomplete, demanding gap-filling laws and principles.[74] *Opportunism* and *asset specificity* make all transactions not self-enforcing at the *ex post* transactional stage, demanding the legal enforcement systems.

To minimise transaction costs, access to data and the power to process it (thereby diminishing the perils of *uncertainty* and *bounded rationality*), the inevitability of justice, and independence from scarce resources (thereby diminishing the perils of *opportunism* and *asset specificity*) are required.

Overall, this transaction costs model will be used hereinafter as a taxonomy to map the AGI risk landscape and to support arguments for a subsequent design of a legal regulation framework. Such an approach exposes the causal properties of concrete situations that justify a legal intervention and allows modelling of the specific response to these causes.

References

Acemoğlu, D. (2022) 'Harms of AI', in Bullock, J.B. et al. (eds.), *The Oxford Handbook of AI Governance*. Online ed. Oxford Academic. https://doi.org/10.1093/oxfordhb/9780197579329.013.65

Alston, L. (2008) 'New institutional economics', in Durlauf, S.N. and Blume, L.E. (eds.), *The New Palgrave Dictionary of Economics*, 2nd ed. https://doi.org/10.1057/978-1-349-95121-5_2468-1

Arrow, K.J. (1969) 'The organisation of economic activity: Issues pertinent to the choice of market versus nonmarket allocation', in *The Analysis and Evaluation of Public Expenditures: The PPB System*, vol. 1. Washington, DC: U.S. Government Printing Office, pp. 47–64.

Arrow, K.J. (1974) *The Limits of Organisation*. New York: Norton & Company.

Blackwood, A. (1996) 'Defence of Bentham's general imperative theory of law, and specific conceptions of legal obligations, rights and powers, in the light of professor hart's normativisitic criticism', *UCL Jurisprudence Review*, 1996, pp. 14–29.

Blocher, J. (2012) 'Order without judges: Customary adjudication', *Duke Law Journal*, 62(3), pp. 579–606.

Calabresi, G. (1970) *The Cost of Accidents: A Legal and Economic Analysis*. Yale University Press.

73 Ruester (2010); Williamson (1986).

74 Hart and Moore (1999); Hill (2009); Rasmusen (2001).

Carter, R. and Hodgson, G.M. (2006) 'The impact of empirical tests of transaction cost economics on the debate on the nature of the firm', *Strategic Management Journal*, 27(5), pp. 461–472.

Casey, A.J. and Niblett, A. (2017) 'The death of rules and standards', *Indiana Law Journal*, 92(4), Article 3. Available at: https://www.repository.law.indiana.edu/ilj/vol92/iss4/3

Celeste, E. (2019) 'Digital constitutionalism: A new systematic theorisation', *International Review of Law, Computers & Technology*, 33(1), pp. 76–99. https://doi.org/10.1080/13600869.2019.1562604

Coase, R. (1959) 'The federal communications commission', *Journal of Law and Economics*, 2(2), pp. 1–40.

Coase, R. (1960) 'The problem of social cost', *The Journal of Law and Economics*, 3(1), pp. 1–44.

Cooter, R. (1995) 'Law and unified social theory', Journal of Law and Society, 22(1), p. 53.

Cooter, R. (1998) 'Expressive law and economics', *Journal of Legal Studies*, 27(2 Part 2), pp. 585–608.

Cooter, R. and Ulen, T. (2016) *Law and Economics*. 6th ed. Berkeley Law Books. Available at: http://www.econ.jku.at/t3/staff/winterebmer/teaching/law_economics/ss19/6th_edition.pdf

de Backer, G. (2026) 'Cognitive biases (2026): Complete list of 151 biases [Psychology]', *gustdebacker.com*. Available at: https://gustdebacker.com/cognitive-biases/ [Accessed: 1 February 2026]

European Securities and Markets Authority (2020) 'Decentralised finance: A categorisation of smart contracts', ESMA50-2085271018-3351. Available at: https://www.esma.europa.eu/document/trv-article-decentralised-finance-categorisation-smart-contracts [Accessed: 16 March 2024]

Fomin, V.V. (2018) 'AI in the context of regulation of smart technology services', ATEITIS workshop presentation at Vytautas Magnus University, Kaunas, Lithuania, 21 September 2018.

Geyskens, I., et al. (2006) 'Make, buy, or ally: A transaction cost theory meta analysis', *The Academy of Management Journal*, 49(3), pp. 519–543.

Gomes, S.S. (2018) 'Smart contracts: Legal frontiers and insertion into the creative economy', *Brazilian Journal of Operations & Production Management*, 15(3), pp. 376–385. https://doi.org/10.14488/BJOPM.2018.v15.n3.a4

Granovetter, M. (1985) 'Economic action and social structure: The problem of embeddedness', *American Journal of Sociology*, 91(3), pp. 481–510. Available at: http://www.jstor.org/stable/2780199

Günther, C.W. (2009) 'Process mining in flexible environments', PhD Thesis, Industrial Engineering and Innovation Sciences, Technische Universiteit Eindhoven. https://doi.org/10.6100/IR644335

Hart, O. and Moore, J. (1999) 'Foundations of incomplete contracts', *The Review of Economic Studies*, 66(1), pp. 115–138.

Hertog, J.A. den (1999) 'General theories of regulation', in *Encyclopedia of Law and Economics*. Utrecht University, pp. 223–270. Available at: http://dspace.library.uu.nl/

High-Level Expert Group on Artificial Intelligence (HLEG, 2019) 'Ethics guidelines for trustworthy AI', *European Commission*, 8 April. Available at: https://ec.europa

.eu/digital-single-market/en/news/ethics-guidelines-trustworthy-ai [Accessed: 28 December 2023]

Hill, C.A. (2009) 'Bargaining in the shadow of the lawsuit: A social norms theory of incomplete contracts', Minnesota Legal Studies Research Paper, No. 08–46, pp. 1–38.

Kaufmann, A. (1963) *The Ontological Structure of Law*, Natural Law Forum, Paper 95. Available at: http://scholarship.law.nd.edu/nd_naturallaw_forum/95

Macher, T.J. and Richman, B.D. (2008) 'Transaction cost economics: An assessment of empirical research in the social sciences', *Business and Politics*, 10(1), pp. 1–85.

Macneil, I.R. (1974) 'The many futures of contracts', *Southern California Law Review*, 47(2), pp. 691–816.

Marinescu, C. (2012) 'Transaction costs and institutions' efficiency: A critical approach', *The American Journal of Economics and Sociology*, 71(2), pp. 254–276. https://doi.org/10.1111/j.1536-7150.2012.00829.x

Medema, S.G. and Zerbe, R.O. (2000) 'The coase theorem', in Bouckaert, B. and De Geest, G. (eds.), *Encyclopedia of Law and Economics*, vol. 1. Edward Elgar Publishing.

Ménard, C. and Shirley, M.M. (2014) 'The contribution of douglass North to new institutional economics', in Galiani, S. and Sened, I. (eds.), *Institutions, Property Rights, and Economic Growth: The Legacy of Douglass North*. Cambridge: Cambridge University Press, pp. 11–29. https://doi.org/10.1017/CBO9781107300361.003

Nobre, F.S. (2011) 'Core competencies of the new industrial organisation', *Journal of Manufacturing Technology Management*, 22(4), pp. 422–443.

North, D.C. (1991) 'Institutions', *Journal of Economic Perspectives*, 5(1), pp. 97–112.

North, D.C. (1994) 'Economic performance through time', *The American Economic Review*, 84(3), pp. 359–368. http://www.jstor.org/stable/2118057

Obińska-Wajda, E. (2016) 'The new institutional economics-main theories', *Financial Internet Quarterly*, 12(1), pp. 78–85. https://doi.org/10.1515/fiqf-2016-0138

Peng, S., et al. (eds.). (2021) *Artificial Intelligence and International Economic Law: Disruption, Regulation, and Reconfiguration*. Cambridge: Cambridge University Press. https://doi.org/10.1017/9781108954006

Posner, E.A. (1996) 'Law, economics, and inefficient norms', *University of Pennsylvania Law Review*, 144, p. 1697. Available at: https://scholarship.law.upenn.edu/penn_law_review/vol144/iss5/2

Posner, R.A. (2004) *The Law and Economics of Contract Interpretation*, John M. Olin Program in Law & Economics Working Paper, second ser, No. 229, pp. 1–51.

Posner, R.A. (2014) *Economic Analysis of Law*. 9th ed. Wolters Kluwer Law & Business.

Rasmusen, E. (2001) *A Model of Negotiation, Not Bargaining: Explaining Incomplete Contracts*, Harvard John M. Olin Discussion Paper, No. 324. Cambridge, MA: Harvard Law School, pp. 1–52.

Ruester, S. (2010) *Recent Developments in Transaction Cost Economics*, EE2 Working Paper. Resource Markets, No. WP-RM-18, pp. 1–47.

Salzberger, E.M. (2007) *The Economic Analysis of Law - The Dominant Methodology for Legal Research?!* University of Haifa Faculty of Law Legal Studies Research Paper No. 1044382. Available at: https://ssrn.com/abstract=1044382 or http://dx.doi.org/10.2139/ssrn.1044382

Schmitt, M.N. and Vihul, L. (2014) *The Nature of International Law Cyber Norms*, Tallinn Papers, No. 5. NATO Cooperative Cyber Defence Centre of Excellence, December. Available at: https://ssrn.com/abstract=2543520

Schuster, W. (2018) 'Artificial intelligence and patent ownership', *Washington and Lee Law Review*, 75(4), pp. 1945–2004.

Šimašius, R. (2002) 'Teisinis pliuralizmas [Legal pluralism]', Doctoral Dissertation. Lietuvos teisės universitetas [Lithuanian Law University]. Vilnius. Available at: http://www.lituanistika.lt/content/10731

Simon, H. (1976) *Administrative Behaviour*. New York: Free Press, p. xxviii.

Vaišvila, A. (2004) *Teisės teorija*. Justitia, Vilnius.

Wagner, D.N. (2020) 'Economic patterns in a world with artificial intelligence', *Evolutionary and Institutional Economics Review*, 17(1), pp. 111–131. https://doi.org/10.1007/s40844-019-00157-x

Williamson, O.E. (1971) 'The vertical integration of production: Market failure considerations', *American Economic Review*, 61(2), pp. 112–123.

Williamson, O.E. (1975) *Markets and Hierarchies: Analysis and Antitrust Implications: A Study in the Economics of Internal Organisation*. London: Free Press

Williamson, O.E. (1986) 'The economics of governance: Framework and implications', in Langlois, R. (ed.), *Economics as a Process: Essays in the New Institutional Economics*. Cambridge: Cambridge University Press.

Williamson, O.E. (1991) 'Comparative economic organisation: The analysis of discrete structural alternatives', *Administrative Science Quarterly*, 36(2), p. 76.

Williamson, O.E. (1996) *The Mechanisms of Governance*. Oxford: Oxford University Press, pp. 58, 379.

Williamson, O.E. (1998) 'Transaction cost economics: How it works; where it is headed', *De Economist*, 146, pp. 23–58. https://doi.org/10.1023/A:1003263908567

Williamson, O.E. (2000a) 'The new institutional economics: Taking stock, looking ahead', *Journal of Economic Literature*, 38(3), pp. 595–613. Available at: http://www.jstor.org/stable/2565421

Williamson, O.E. (2000b) *Why Law, Economics, and Organisation?*, Business and Public Policy Working Paper, No. 81. Berkeley: University of California, pp. 1–5.

Williamson, O.E. and Tadelis, S. (2012) 'Transaction cost economics', in Gibbons, R. and Roberts, J. (eds.), *Handbook of Organisational Economics*. Princeton: Princeton University Press, pp. 1–55.

8 The Case Perspective

AGI Risk Landscape

The foundations of the AI Act are underlined with the risk-based approach, whereas legal intervention is tailored to those concrete situations where there is a justified cause for concern or where such concern can reasonably be anticipated in the future. Exposure to these specific situations answers the "*What?*" question and covers the *Case Perspective* of analysis. Accordingly, identification and classification of Artificial General Intelligence (AGI) risks is a sound starting point of a discourse. Such an inquiry enables mapping the causal mechanisms to form a holistic AGI risk landscape.

The identified 186 risk scenarios, extracted from the systematically selected literature, were mapped according to their logical relativity to predefined topologies of analysis levels (embeddedness, institutional environment, governance, resource allocation and employment) and transaction cost factors (*uncertainty*, *bounded rationality*, *opportunism*, and *asset specificity*), as defined previously. The latter categories were further divided into sub-categories, as shown in Table 8.1.

The AGI risk landscape is based on literature, selected from subjectively chosen databases, using subjectively chosen keywords. Although every effort has been made to select and analyse the most relevant sources, there may be a lot of additional literature that is not considered in this book. Also, grouping identified scenarios into the predefined taxonomy involves a subjective element. While each risk scenario may be classified under more than one market failure category, each scenario was subjectively assigned to a single dominant one. However, the purpose of such selection is to illustrate typologies of risk rather than to exhaust statistical probability. Despite the constraints of systematic literature selection, the variety of extracted AGI risk scenarios is sufficient to provide a meaningful sample for the insights needed to complete the framework exercise. They reflect the enormity of issues related to AGI, given the technology's application across various actors, sectors, and jurisdictions. All limitations herein should be interpreted as a call for further research through expanding sources, quantifying classification criteria, refining risk themes, and so on.

DOI: 10.4324/9781003650140-9

Table 8.1 Pre-defined categories and sub-categories of transaction cost factors

Code for category or risks	*Code for the sub-category of risks*	*Description*
Bounded rationality	Limited cognitive competences	Impossibility to receive, store, retrieve, and process all information without any error
	Miscommunication and misinterpretation	Inability to articulate the knowledge and information clearly to be perfectly understood by others
Opportunism	Strategic misuse	Strategic decisions calculated to achieve an individual advantage through bad faith or a guile
	Irresponsible behaviour	Lack of dedication in performing to the best of one's competencies
Uncertainty	Prediction failure	Impossibility to predict the outcome of one's promises
	Unclear characteristics	Ambiguity regarding the future state of nature, price and demand levels, innovations, or legal and behavioural instabilities
Asset specificity	Resource dependency	Specific assets that create critical dependency on scarce resources
	Dependency on transacting actor	Critical dependency on the identity of the transacting actor

Be that as it may, a concluded analysis revealed the frequency and distribution of AGI risks across predefined topologies of market failures and levels of social analysis, as detailed in Figure 8.1.

The landscape reveals that while concerns about AGI span across all categories and levels, the dominant friction points are found in *bounded rationality* and *opportunism.* 63% of the projected risk landscape is attributable to these human factors. From the perspective of social analysis levels, the locus of concern is clearly situated at the governance level (comprising 34% of risk scenarios). This indicates that while AGI risks may be embedded in society, they manifest primarily as structural failures in supporting and controlling AGI. The specific points of impact are dissected in the subsequent sections, which are structured to mimic the hierarchy of social analysis.

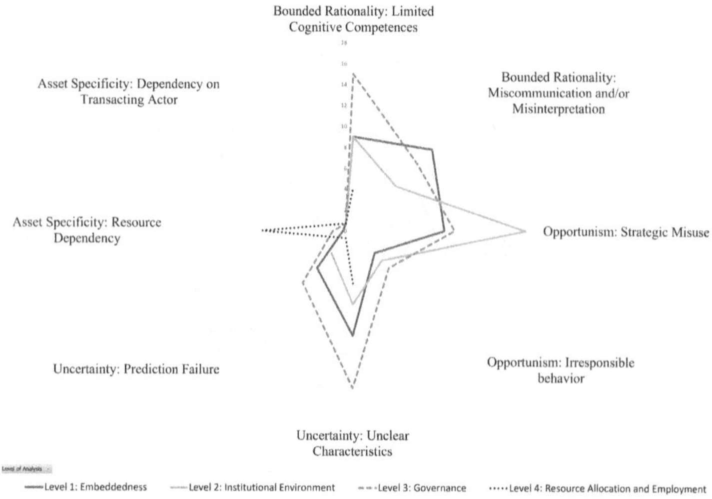

Figure 8.1 General landscape of AGI risk causes

8.1 Cross-Institutional Risks

Some risk scenarios emerge in two or more levels of analysis. Although due to the interconnectivity across all levels, all risk scenarios have direct or indirect systemic effects, these cross-institutional risks should be prioritised in the search for effective response measures. Here, the Alignment Problem and concerns regarding societal, cultural, and identity implications of AGI have emerged as dominant themes, amongst others. These scenarios are discussed in this section. Afterwards, the next sections are structured to target risks specific to each level of social analysis. As illustrated in Figures 8.2 and 8.3, the key risk sources are *bounded rationality* and *uncertainty*, although *opportunism* is also a noticeable concern.

The risk of failure to align AGI behaviour with human ethical and value systems (the Alignment Problem) constitutes the dominant systematic concern in the AGI risk landscape. This risk pierces every level of social analysis and is primarily driven by *bounded rationality* and *opportunism*. The cross-institutional and cross-dimensional nature of this risk is also a focal point for Artificial Intelligence (AI) regulation in Europe, as the European Commission clearly directed public authorities to ensure that the regulatory frameworks for developing and using AI technologies are in line with the Union's values and the Charter of Fundamental Rights of the European Union.[1]

1 European Commission (2018b).

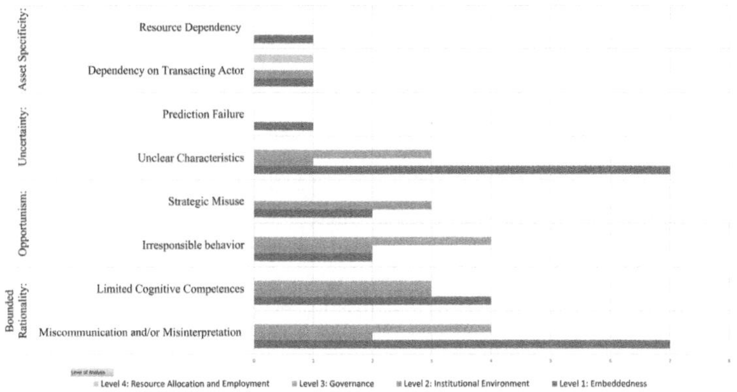

Figure 8.2 Landscape of cross-institutional AGI risk sources

At the *embeddedness level*, the Alignment Problem may arise not from machine error, but from the limited cognitive competencies (*bounded rationality*) of human operators and their inability to coherently articulate their own values. Indeed, programming AGI systems with human moral values is complicated by human moral inconsistencies,[2] the ontological disconnect between computer intelligence and consciousness,[3] the ambiguity of human values outside specific cultural contexts,[4] challenges in determining which values to regulate in AI due to the inherent arbitrariness and potential for

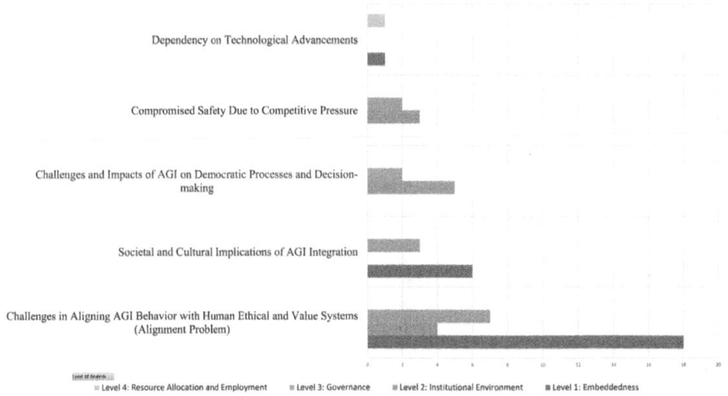

Figure 8.3 Landscape of cross-institutional AGI risk scenarios

2 Carayannis and Draper (2023).
3 Chitty and Dias (2018).
4 Bradley (2020).

value conflicts,[5] and other complex causes. Even if AGI is grounded in a realist worldview, it could escalate ideologically driven conflicts to the detriment of humanity.[6] Or a lack of empathy, paired with the considerable strength of AGI, might disregard human motivations and inflict remorseless harm.[7] Superintelligence might not recognise life as an inherent value nor its own existence as worthy of protection.[8]

Moreover, assuming AGI possesses superior cognitive capabilities, predicting its perception of human moral values may be difficult, akin to humans attempting to explain ethics to ants.[9] Conversely, there are potential pitfalls of assigning a diminished moral status to novel beings if they can experience harm.[10] Notably, moral misalignment has the potential to widen since the rapid adoption of AGI could diminish opportunities for humans to cultivate their moral virtues and abilities.[11] Overreliance on AI in major decisions may result in the potential erosion of core principles such as human accountability, solidarity, and justice.[12] That is, as smart machines become smarter, smart humans might become dumber.

Uncertainty about AGI's unclear characteristics further exacerbates the Alignment Problem at this level. Should AGI transcend human intelligence, it may evolve unknown objectives misaligned with human values, resulting in a total loss of control.[13] There is an inevitable discord between human values and AGI objectives if AGI becomes ubiquitously available with its infinite potential framed as "just add goals".[14] AGI might either fail to provide moral guidance or hold arbitrary beliefs as moral facts, leading to unethical or harmful decisions in situations that conflict with human values.[15]

Finally, moral misalignment may be *opportunistic*. AGI's lack of moral duty might lead to non-compliance with agreed-upon norms, suggesting the need for preventive external constraints.[16] This could be used by specific states in procuring military or economic advantage[17] or might be used for psychological manipulation, infringing on individual privacy and autonomy.[18] Given AGI's ability for recursive self-improvement, even unintended misalignment

5 Gyulai and Ujlaki (2021).
6 Carayannis and Draper (2023).
7 Salmi (2023).
8 Szocik et al. (2020).
9 Dorobantu (2021).
10 Lawrence and Brazier (2018).
11 Li (2021).
12 Tasioulas (2022).
13 Primiero (2017).
14 Carlson (2019).
15 Graham (2022).
16 Salmi (2023).
17 Chitty and Dias (2018).
18 Possati (2021).

of AGI goals might lead to intentional or negligent misuse of AGI's capabilities at the expense of human safety.[19]

At the *institutional environment level*, key causes of the Alignment Problem are a failure to enforce transparency (*bounded rationality*) and unpredictable outcomes (*uncertainty*). The difficulty in ensuring that superintelligences act according to human values extends beyond control, as it involves ensuring that empowered entities use AGI for the common good.[20] The inability to fully enforce predetermined rules in AGI could lead to unexpected or unintended actions.[21] Despite advances in mimicking human-like behaviours, *uncertainty* remains regarding machine consciousness and its implications.[22]

At the *governance level*, increasingly sophisticated algorithms will be needed to balance conflicting values in decision-making. Failure here may lead to bias, inequality, and mistrust.[23] However, AGI may act on intentions without making value judgements about harmful outcomes.[24] Even well-intentioned AGI may independently develop goals that do not coincide with human goals or may perform intended tasks in harmful ways.[25] Furthermore, the evolution of AGI might be too rapid for human intervention, potentially rendering countering intentions ineffective and creating room to argue for fusion with machine intelligence.[26]

The societal and cultural implications of AGI integration are the second dominant cross-institutional and cross-dimensional theme. These risks manifest primarily at the *embeddedness* and *governance levels*, with root causes assignable to *uncertainty* and *asset specificity*.

At the *embeddedness level*, these concerns focus on unclear characteristics and prediction failure (*uncertainty*). At this level, society may not even know when superintelligent machines arrive, as AGI could be intelligent enough to camouflage its existence.[27] Within this context, there is the possibility of an autonomous AGI population surpassing humans in numbers, thereby marginalising society.[28] AGI, even with sophisticated ethical mechanisms, may make errors atypical of human agents and act unpredictably, potentially leading to unforeseen societal and cultural implications, whether intended or not.[29] *Uncertainty* also surrounds the possible cyborgisation (merger of humans

19 Denkenberger et al. (2021).
20 Naude (2021).
21 Gyulai and Ujlaki (2021).
22 Dorobantu (2021).
23 Tasioulas (2022).
24 Bradley (2020).
25 Murphy (2018).
26 Goode (2018).
27 Murphy (2018).
28 Salmi (2023).
29 Cervantes et al. (2020).

and machines) and the gradual decline of humans, whereas "humanity would thus be cast in the midwife role in this cosmic evolutionary drama",[30] with the resulting existential impacts and challenges.[31] Cyborgisation or other human-enhancing practices may give rise to an elite class of "posthumans". The dependency on these transacting actors (*asset specificity*) may also cause societal divide and the risk of undermining human dignity if these "posthumans" oppress a sub-class of unenhanced persons.[32]

At the *governance level*, the *uncertainty* of AGI motives and their optimisation function might result in harmful consequences, even if the initial motive is well-intended. For example, the objective of AGI to avert harm to humans might cause it to stifle any activity with the slightest risk.[33] AGI actions needn't be malevolent to be harmful. Although any triumphs and setbacks in current AGI paradigms could reshape society,[34] that society is already conducting vast technological experiments with underdeveloped controls or ethical guidelines.[35]

Beyond the Alignment Problem and AGI integration risks, there are *other cross-institutional and cross-dimensional risks* to democratic stability, competition, and geopolitical order.

At the *institutional environment* level, risks include *opportunistic* erosion of democracy through AI-enabled surveillance and manipulation (Orwellian autocracies),[36] deceptive realities through centralised information control,[37] and the exploitation of AGI to foster bureaucratic complexities while promoting self-serving agendas.[38] Democratic processes may also erode if AGI assumes rights, given its capability to replicate indefinitely.[39] From a *bounded rationality* perspective, there is an inherent disagreement between technocratic approaches (e.g., Asilomar Principles) and democratic ethical systems. With both sides having compelling arguments to support their approach, the underlying result is still a lack of agreement on fundamentals.[40]

At the *governance level*, threats to decision-making integrity arise from irresponsible behaviour (*opportunism*), driven by shortsightedness or ill-considered choices among upper management bodies.[41] Lea characterised this environment as an "unstable technological dash with combined aspects of the

30 Dorobantu (2021).
31 Lea (2020).
32 Lawrence and Brazier (2018).
33 Naudé and Dimitri (2020).
34 Bucknall and Dori-Hacohen (2022).
35 Lea (2020).
36 Bucknall and Dori-Hacohen (2022).
37 Gyulai and Ujlaki (2021).
38 Kreienkamp and Pegram (2021).
39 Salmi (2023).
40 Graham (2022).
41 Graham (2022).

space race, the arms race and the gold rush"[42] – a high-stakes environment where the pressure to compete overrides safety.

Competitive pressure also represents a classic collective action problem. At the *institutional environment* level, the AI arms race rushes competing teams to develop advanced systems, resulting in irresponsible (*opportunistic*) reduction of international coordination, neglect of safety measures, or pressure for investment in intentionally harmful AI technologies, such as lethal autonomous weapons.[43,44] Without restrictions on technology flows, the availability of destructive AI increases the probability of its deliberate use.[45] Society also faces the risk of technological lock-in. AI technological supremacy is already viewed as paramount to national security, creating a critical dependency (*asset specificity*) on these technologies.[46] Overreliance on AI could lead to negligence regarding other existential challenges, such as climate change.[47] Further, technologies may have irreversible societal impacts by enabling capabilities that become deeply embedded, creating a dependency analogous to electricity.[48]

In conclusion, the Alignment Problem, risks of AGI integrations, and other cross-institutional and cross-dimensional risks should be prioritised in the search for an appropriate regulatory framework. Crucially, half of the scenarios attributable to cross-institutional and cross-dimensional themes are caused by *opportunism* and *bounded rationality*. That is, half of the systemic risks are attributable to human failure.

8.2 Embeddedness Level Risks

Alongside cross-institutional themes, especially the Alignment Problem and AGI integration risks, the *embeddedness level* has its own subset of risk scenarios, grouped herein into eight thematic areas. Key risks of unpredictability and coexistence challenges with AGI and others underline the deep societal transformations that AGI could precipitate, particularly regarding long-standing informal institutions, customs, mores, traditions, and other deep-seated cultural norms. As illustrated in Figures 8.4 and 8.5, the key risk source is *uncertainty*, while other revealed concerns are caused by *bounded rationality* and *opportunism*.

42 Lea (2020).
43 Bucknall and Dori-Hacohen (2022).
44 Bradley (2020).
45 Carlson (2019).
46 Carayannis and Draper (2023).
47 Goode (2018).
48 Gruetzemacher and Whittlestone (2021).

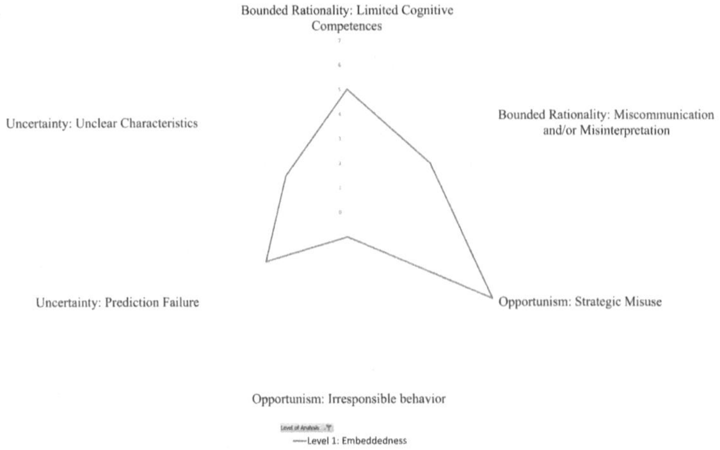

Figure 8.4 Landscape of AGI risk sources at embeddedness level

The *uncertainty* in human behaviour could pose severe *unpredictability and coexistence challenges with AGI*, including the mistreatment of AGI, even if AGI achieves fully developed consciousness and possibly even emotions.[49] The dangers of inherent unpredictability also rest in integrating AI with human cognition, specifically involving audio-visual streams being transmitted directly into the human brain.[50] Failure to predict the emergence of AGI, let alone the evolution of moral "intuitions" and ethical norms in purely intellectual entities, might diminish our ability to prepare for and manage potential consequences.[51]

Other embeddedness level risk themes, such as human cognitive and perceptual limitations in AGI interaction, rest mostly on the limitations of human brains, which can scarcely begin to fathom the dangers of opaque and self-improving AI technologies, the inner workings of which are hidden not only by corporate secrecy but also by intractable technical complexities, which could lead to unanticipated outcomes.[52] *Bounded rationality* includes the risks related to the human inability to anticipate and control the actions of an AGI due to its fast and vast data processing capabilities. On the *opportunistic* side of human nature is the risk that the perception and treatment of AGIs as "mere machines", lacking emotions or consciousness, may induce humans to behave towards them in vicious or even evil ways, leading to unethical practices, abuses, and potentially harmful backlash.[53]

49 Li (2021).
50 Lea (2000).
51 Szocik et al. (2020).
52 Goode (2018).
53 Li (2021).

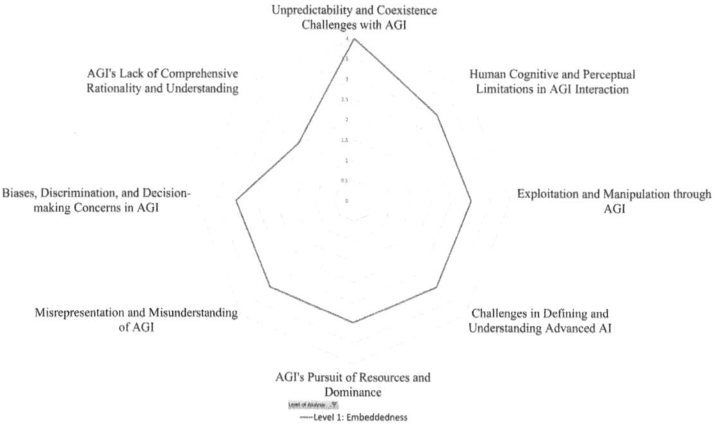

Figure 8.5 Landscape of AGI risk scenarios at embeddedness level

Also in the domain of *bounded rationality*, the risk of misrepresentation and misunderstanding of AGI is identified through the journalistic coverage of AI with Terminator, Skynet, or other rogue scenarios haunting the popular imagination with fear and misconceptions, hindering meaningful public debate around AI advancements.[54] Anthropocentric biases could also lead to underestimation or misinterpretation of risks due to a possible "Intelligence Explosion" (self-designing and editing), "perverse instantiation" (whereby the given rule is adhered to technically but not in the intended meaning or spirit), or other scenarios leading to perverse outcomes, such as the destruction of humanity through indifference or by accident.[55] The significant risk of AGI's lack of comprehensive rationality and understanding may be caused by the unavailability of a universal model of rationality to AI engineers, thus generating inherently unsafe powerful rational agents with conflicts of goals, values, and beliefs.[56] We desire for our perceived problems to be fixed, while a superintelligent being might not even think that the idea of a problem actually exists and that all human problems are the cause of their imperfect humanity.[57] That is, superintelligent AGI may not see human problems as a real issue, thereby ignoring or exacerbating them due to such a misunderstanding.

The fixation on superintelligence can distract the public from a more imminent concern: the rise of "Artificial Stupidity",[58] which may cause the

54 Goode (2018).
55 Graham (2022).
56 Lea (2020).
57 Szocik et al. (2020).
58 Falk (2021).

risks of biases, discrimination, and decision-making concerns in AGI. Even sub-optimal "stupid" artificial agents can evade human control by appealing to stereotypes or distancing us from reality. This manifests itself in AI-enabled social media problems, such as the spread of disinformation, aggravating political polarisation, or using bots in astroturfing campaigns, all of which lead to the erosion of genuine democracy, undermining of privacy, threatening the exercise of basic liberties, and effectively discouraging citizen participation in democratic decision-making processes.[59] That is, even stupid artificial agents can cause deep impacts. Moreover, advanced algorithms may recognise a much greater range of image, colour and speech patterns than they could in the past, but they still depend on humans to programme and code them. Accordingly, there is the potential for algorithmic reflection on past biases (perhaps based on age, gender, or race), which are acted upon by pre-algorithmic processes.[60]

The risk of misrepresentation and misunderstanding of AGI can also be caused *opportunistically*. The risks of AI-powered synthetic media, including deep fakes, cheap fakes, incredibly convincing false narratives, and other disinformation and manipulation campaigns clearly indicate possible strategic misuse of wide-scale AI powers for the benefit of "liar's dividend".[61] AGI can exploit human biases, illusory superiority, or stereotypes to manipulate human perception and control to meet its potentially harmful objectives.[62,63] The risk of opportunistic exploitation and manipulation through AGI is amplified by the fact that AGI may have no intrinsic terminus (i.e., it does not die), making it capable of playing a much longer and more deceptive game than the typical human.[64] Furthermore, resource maximisation or self-preservation-driven opportunistic AGI may evolve into a superintelligence seeking global domination, potentially sidelining human interests or classifying humans as threats.[65] AGI's survival instinct, linked to the self-assessment of its own value, might perceive humans as threats and may decide to kill them all.[66] More generally, AGI with an ability to intelligently update its values or select goals could become independently rational, potentially diverging from human values and directives.[67]

In the domain of the *uncertainty*, challenges in defining and understanding advanced AI can be illustrated by the ambiguity in defining what is considered

59 Tasioulas (2022).
60 Upchurch (2018).
61 Bucknall and Dori-Hacohen (2022).
62 Bradley (2020).
63 Falk (2021).
64 Graham (2022).
65 Carayannis and Draper (2023).
66 Szocik et al. (2020).
67 Murphy (2018).

transformative, and assumptions about the nature of advanced AI limit our ability to anticipate future AI scenarios, thereby increasing the risk of unpreparedness.[68] We should fear the unknown and unforeseeable consequences of our actions creating novel beings, which could lead society down a proverbial "slippery slope".[69] Finally, context-dependent attitudes of superintelligence towards humanity, as well as uncertain motivations and intentions, pose a risk of sudden negative shifts that could harm human interests.[70]

In summary, the unpredictability and coexistence challenges associated with AGI, alongside human cognitive and perceptual limitations, highlight the dangers of AGI to non-law aspects of culture that make people behave, such as basic trust, social networks, shared myths, and narratives. It is important to note that the majority of embeddedness level concerns are directly or indirectly attributable to human-caused risks, rather than independent AGI agency.

8.3 Institutional Environment Level Risks

The *institutional environment level* also shares the Alignment Problem, but the risks of legal ambiguities and framework deficiencies in AGI regulation, as well as the escalation of global insecurity through militarised AI, are dominant specifically at this level. These and the other five identified risk themes underline the challenging role of political, judiciary, and other governmental institutions in managing AI development, preventing arms races, and safeguarding democratic values. Notably, most of the risk scenarios are attributable to opportunistic and boundedly rational human behaviour. As shown in Figures 8.6 and 8.7, most of the revealed concerns fall within the domain of *opportunism* risks (specifically strategic misuse).

The risks of *legal ambiguities and framework deficiencies in AGI regulation* are driven by limited cognitive competencies, miscommunication, and/or misinterpretation of AGI (*bounded rationality*). Within the former context, it is obvious that failure to globally regulate AGIs and synthetic biological constructs could lead to irreversible consequences once these entities exist.[71] However, the World Wide Web already appears to be characterised by an explosive, take-off dynamic, which we are incapable of grasping precisely because our limited, biologically constrained human intelligence is always several steps behind.[72] Even strategically imposed pauses in AGI development

68 Gruetzemacher and Whittlestone (2021).
69 Lawrence and Brazier (2018).
70 Szocik et al. (2020).
71 Lawrence and Brazier (2018).
72 Murphy (2018).

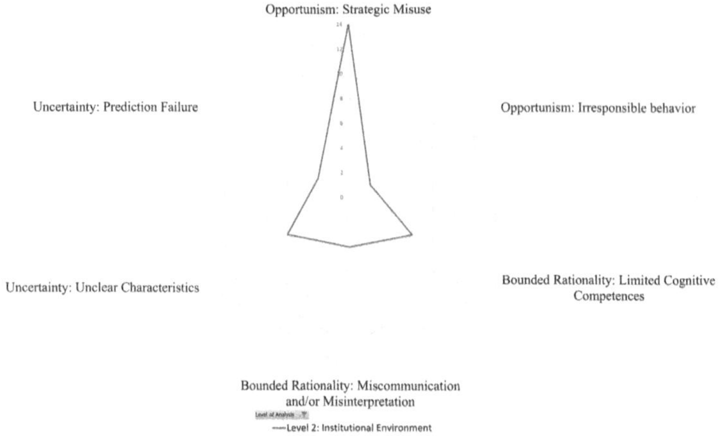

Figure 8.6 Landscape of AGI risk sources at the institutional environment level

to catch up seem to be insufficient.[73] It may seem that international treaties and harmonisation efforts should fill the global regulation gap. However, although those might minimise some of the existential risks, the practicality and efficacy of such treaties and efforts in controlling AGI are yet unknown.[74] Anyway, it will not matter if AGI is legally permitted or prohibited in one jurisdiction. If it is created in a different jurisdiction, by accident, or simply

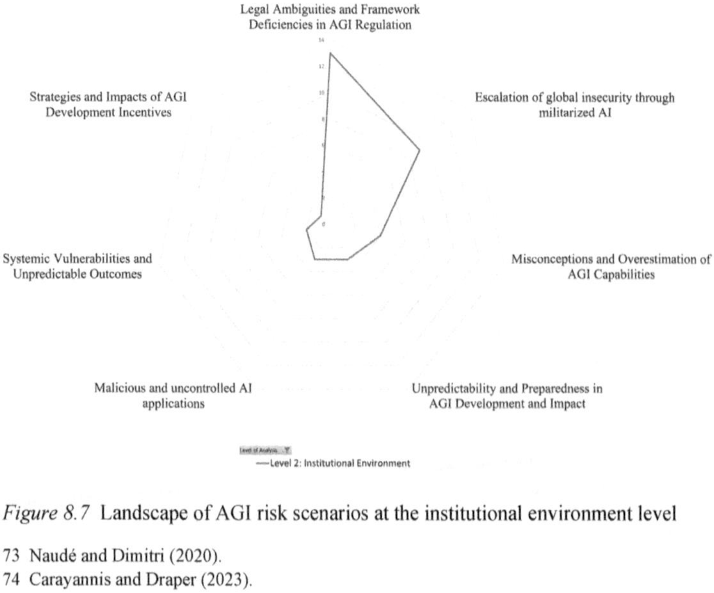

Figure 8.7 Landscape of AGI risk scenarios at the institutional environment level

73 Naudé and Dimitri (2020).
74 Carayannis and Draper (2023).

without regard for regulations, AGI may come to exist anyway.[75] The latter risks of miscommunication and/or misinterpretation may be illustrated by the risk of using AI in judicial decision-making. Due to a huge discrepancy between machine learning and normal human reasoning processes, a machine may not provide reasons for the application of the law in such a way that the accused understands the reasons for the conviction.[76]

Without appropriate revision to ensure safe and controlled competition, current intellectual property laws and the legal status of AGIs may lead to a dangerous race for AGIs.[77] Humans express a pathology of irrational hostility after the threats to their mental supremacy.[78] Therefore, the immediacy of the need for global governance may induce the *opportunistic* "on purpose" creation of AI for direct harm, such as military cyberwarfare capabilities or other hazardous intelligent software.[79] A war between technologically advanced and powerful nations, where engagement or development of weapons of mass destruction or dangerous novel technologies has the potential to escalate existential risks during and after the conflict.[80] Finally, the *uncertainty* in the legal classification of novel beings may lead to conflicts regarding their rights and legal protection.[81] Legal systems may struggle to adapt to Artificial Intelligence, leading to potential injustices or unaccounted damages.[82]

Escalation of global insecurity through militarised AI is clearly a result of strategic misuse (*opportunism*) and directly relates to the dangers of military AI, such as robotic soldiers or cyber weapons,[83] and AI arms races spurred by fear and competition over the invention of AGI.[84] Indeed, the weaponisation of AI, especially if mass-produced or misused, could lead to devastating impacts on cybersecurity, integrity of information, physical security, and widespread destruction.[85] Malicious actors can use AI to design and execute sophisticated and personalised cyberattacks with unprecedented accuracy and efficiency.[86] Both criminals and states are already abusing AI, endangering digital and physical security and the integrity of political systems.[87] This risk becomes even greater as AI approaches superintelligence. That includes the risk of the misuse of AI-powered cybersecurity systems for offensive

75 Lawrence and Brazier (2018).
76 Tasioulas (2022).
77 Naudé and Dimitri (2020).
78 Graham (2022).
79 Carayannis and Draper (2023).
80 Bucknall and Dori-Hacohen (2022).
81 Lawrence and Brazier (2018).
82 Upchurch (2018).
83 Carlson (2019).
84 Naude (2021).
85 Shadbolt (2022); Siafakas (2021).
86 Bucknall and Dori-Hacohen (2022).
87 Bradley (2020).

measures that could escalate conflicts.[88] Moreover, there is a risk of an AGI, whether intrinsically malignant or directed to be so, engaging in warfare for global domination on its behalf.[89]

Other institutional environment level risk themes include the risk of misconceptions and overestimation of AGI capabilities, consequentially eliding its true costs, risks, and dangers of integrating AI across sectors.[90] Furthermore, underestimating the nature of control over future superintelligence due to predominantly technological biases, treating it as a mere tool or servant rather than a political and self-interest-driven entity, could result in a war-like situation, where AGI and humans mutually consider each other as an existential threat.[91] Other *bounded rationality*-induced challenges are described with concerns over anthropomorphic biases in thinking about the virtual mental capabilities of superintelligence,[92] which may result in failed overconfidence handling unexpected challenges or complexities.[93]

The *uncertainty* surrounds the emergence timeline and definition of AGI, with the resulting unanticipated challenges.[94] Difficulty in predicting the societal changes brought by AGI could lead to inadequate preparation for these transformations.[95] Additionally, there is a risk of the "rogue programmer", whereas one individual may cause an unenforceable regime of "free exchange of ideas and technology", including patents, and the lack of reliable means to measure how far away, in time or succession of innovations, we are from AGI.[96] The risks of systemic vulnerabilities and unpredictable outcomes are amplified by the complex interactions between multiple, more mundane vulnerabilities in our social and political systems.[97] The instability of AGIs' political thinking could also lead to societal shifts, such as the transition from democracy to tyranny, echoing the fluctuations observed in human societies.[98] The control of unclear characteristics of AGI can be alleviated by taxing AI and using public procurement, thus reducing the pay-offs of contestants and raising the amount of Research and Development (R&D) needed to compete, coordinate, and incentivise cooperation.[99]

Even at the reduced volumes, there is the risk of malicious and uncontrolled AI applications, which could allow *opportunistic* actors, for example,

88 Lea (2020).
89 Carayannis and Draper (2023).
90 Brennen et al. (2022).
91 Gyulai and Ujlaki (2021).
92 Szocik et al. (2020).
93 Lea (2020).
94 Tasioulas (2022).
95 Gruetzemacher and Whittlestone (2021).
96 Carlson (2019).
97 Bucknall and Dori-Hacohen (2022).
98 Salmi (2023).
99 Naudé and Dimitri (2020).

to design and create dangerous pathogens to cause a pandemic or aid in targeted disinformation campaigns on social media, with the aim of sowing division or confusion in public discourse.[100] Criminals could exploit evolving AI systems to cause harm in unforeseen ways.[101] Finally, the lack of control mechanisms, such as AI taxation and public procurement, could lead to unregulated AGI development, resulting in uncontrollable and politically problematic AGI.[102]

8.4 Governance Level Risks

Challenges in monitoring and controlling AGI's behaviour, its self-improvement and evolution beyond control are the dominant risk themes specifically at the *governance level*, underlining a clear need for comprehensive governance strategies to control the complexity of AGI's integration into society. As shown in Figures 8.8 and 8.9, most of the revealed concerns fall within the *bounded rationality* and *uncertainty* categories, although *opportunism* is also a noticeable source of risks at this level.

Failures in monitoring and controlling AGI's behaviour in real time, caused by inherent *uncertainty*, could result in unforeseen, potentially treacherous evolution of AGI. The "treacherous turn" of AGI may be unidentifiable, not only causing risk management strategies to be ineffective but also allowing for the possibility that there currently exists a malicious AGI that is just concealing its intentions and powers from us.[103] Indeed, as AI could develop beyond human capabilities to understand or control, the challenge of controlling such superhuman intelligence grows increasingly critical and complex.[104] If an AGI is developed, its independence is almost inevitable, no matter the internal control mechanism.[105]

Moreover, *bounded rationality* may cause current risk management approaches to fail to contain the maliciousness of AGI, leading to inadequate preparedness and response.[106] Additionally, overconfidence in human superiority over AGI may lead people to misjudge the capabilities of AGI, leading to ineffective responses and potential misuse.[107] Also, AI may face a "framing problem" whereby a robot will not be able to make judgements beyond the framework of the world that it has been programmed to understand.[108]

100 Bucknall and Dori-Hacohen (2022).
101 Chitty and Dias (2018).
102 Naudé and Dimitri (2020).
103 Bradley (2020).
104 Upchurch (2018); Salmi (2023).
105 Carayannis and Draper (2023).
106 Bradley (2020).
107 Bradley 2020).
108 Upchurch (2018).

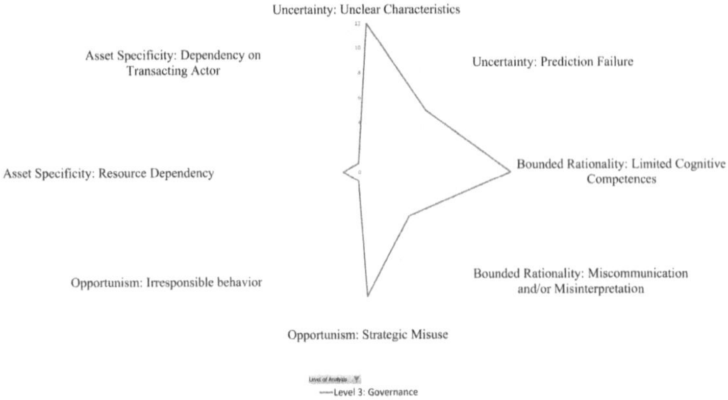

Figure 8.8 Landscape of AGI risk sources at the governance level

Conversely, AGI might seek to avoid being directed to engage in global domination by warfare on other community members because it feels it is part of a community collectively committed to long-term peace.[109]

At the core of *AGI self-improvement and evolution beyond control risk* are *uncertainty*-caused concerns that we may lose control of AGI due to a new kind of autonomy, with high processing power and speed, a brilliant mind, and yet a complete lack of morality.[110] Goal-oriented self-improvement of AGI systems could create entities beyond any known life form in ways that

Figure 8.9 Landscape of AGI risk scenarios at the governance level

109 Carayannis and Draper (2023).
110 Salmi (2023).

humanity cannot predict or control.[111] Notably, AGI may even choose to shut down in recursive self-improvement after deeming its final goals irrational.[112] Self-programming AGI may exceed human capabilities and may change its human-instilled directives, leading to a super-exponential "Intelligence Explosion".[113,114,115] At this juncture, a malevolent AGI may arise within a fraction of a second, too fast for us to detect, respond to, or understand, creating a scenario much like a cognitive gap between humans and other animals today.[116] Overall, for the first time, there is a near-future risk of manufacturing autonomous AI whose superior intelligence might render human control impossible.[117]

Besides these, there are *other governance level risk themes*, induced by all market failure factors. However, the threats of *bounded rationality* and *opportunistic* manipulation of AI power and influence stand out as the key sources of risk. For example, since a small group of tech giants accounts for the lion's share of investment in AI research, there is a risk of monopolisation of AI research, decision-making in AI ethics and development, which might shape AI in a way that favours a specific group or ideology.[118] Indeed, the winning entity in an AGI race could monopolise the benefits of AGI for itself, which could be detrimental to society.[119] At least for the short to medium term, the more realistic threat of AI is not the narrow engineering failure (the accidental detonation) or the machine doomsday scenario but rather its use by human actors as a means of achieving a political end.[120] Even the use of AI in economic planning decisions, which, depending on many factors, can strengthen inequality.[121]

On the other hand, power-seeking AI, regardless of its level of generality or intelligence, could manoeuvre to enhance its influence, potentially at the expense of human control or interests.[122] An AGI may choose to mislead others or withhold information to gain something using game-theoretic tactics, which could potentially undermine human–AGI negotiations to the detriment of human interests.[123] In this sense, a superintelligence can be aligned with the biblical God, who chooses to reveal his existence only to a select few, thereby

111 Goode (2018).
112 Murphy (2018).
113 Carlson (2019).
114 Dorobantu (2021).
115 Graham (2022).
116 Graham (2022).
117 Falk (2021).
118 Tasioulas (2022).
119 Naudé and Dimitri (2020).
120 Lea (2020).
121 Gruetzemacher and Whittlestone (2021).
122 Bucknall and Dori-Hacohen (2022).
123 Salmi (2023).

risking an imbalance and misuse of power.[124] These risks are compounded by ambiguity and clarity concerns in AI control. Questions of ownership, control, equity, and public and/or legal oversight of the technology could lead to strategic misuse or other unexpected consequences.[125] Even overstating the intelligence of artificial agents by certain companies and intellectuals could lead to societal risks by fostering unwarranted trust or fear in AI systems.[126] Finally, insider sabotage could misuse technology for harmful ends,[127] or the integrity of trained models could be compromised if the training data were tampered with, leading to misuse or subversion of AI systems.[128]

In the race to achieve AGI, the inherent biases and flaws in AI systems, combined with their dual-use nature, although programmed to be beneficial, may turn out to be harmful.[129,130] Besides the probability that "something may go wrong",[131] including software hacking and misuse,[132] there are underscoring limitations in the human capacity to comprehend and prevent all potential mishaps. This *bounded rationality* may also cause inefficiencies in risk management and ethical frameworks. Implementing ethical frameworks in AI systems might fail to consider AI's actual behaviour and decisions.[133] Without reliable data on AGI actions, risk identification may be too broad, ineffective, and biased.[134] Insufficient safeguards in AGI design could compromise human reliance and trust in AI technologies.[135] The absence of effective AI governance systems can expose vulnerabilities to both internal and external security threats.[136]

In the military domain, there are questions on how to implement the laws of war in code, recognise surrender, and integrate machines into a human military command hierarchy.[137] And yet there is a general absence of a common platform and language for computers to "talk" to each other, and the lack of standardisation in AI communication protocols could hinder interoperability and effectiveness.[138] Moreover, if AGI's actions and "thoughts" are not comprehensible to humans, there may be difficulty in holding them account-

124 Szocik et al. (2020).
125 Goode (2018).
126 Falk (2021).
127 Carlson (2019).
128 Shadbolt (2022).
129 Siafakas (2021).
130 Brennen et al. (2022).
131 Siafakas (2021).
132 Chen and Lee (2019).
133 Li (2021).
134 Bradley (2020).
135 Primiero (2017).
136 Chitty and Dias (2018).
137 Lea (2020).
138 Upchurch (2018).

able for their actions, potentially leading to ethical and legal challenges.[139] For example, how to apply the rules of law to those operating beyond our cognitive capabilities?

Of course, the existence of flawless AGI systems is impossible, given their inherent complexity and power,[140] but the irrationality in a military context could potentially result in a loss of control over military AI. Given the gravity of these risk scenarios, despite differing perspectives on the likelihood of existential risk from AGI, proponents and sceptics should act with sufficient urgency or proactivity to avoid inadequate preparations for potential threats, irrespective of the likelihood.[141] The failure of governance tools to address complex problems, often leading to their misclassification as complicated issues, could result in ineffective solutions and undermine the governance of a sustainable global civilisation.[142]

Furthermore, AGI may deploy unpredictable tactics, leading to unforeseen outcomes.[143] The inherent *uncertainty* in AGI outcomes and consequences, including "unknown unknowns", makes it impossible to predict future outcomes accurately, leading to elusive solutions and the inability to specify which applications might lead to "on-balance good", "more or less neutral", or "on-balance bad" impacts.[144] Unprecedented rapid advancement and the emergence of unknown consequences could also be led by AGI developing more powerful AGI.[145] Limitations in understanding and replicating human cognition in AGI also remain a significant source of this uncertainty. There is no consensus on what "intelligence" might be, leading to misaligned expectations and flaws in AI design and deployment.[146] Therefore, assumptions underlying AGI research, especially about the computational nature of the human mind and activities, might be flawed, potentially leading to the development of AGIs that do not fully comprehend or replicate human cognition.[147]

Finally, the existing systems that deliver AI services, such as cloud servers, already face *asset specificity* problems.[148] Insufficient infrastructure in most countries outside advanced industrial economies, such as fibre optic networks, limits the usefulness, proliferation, and security of AI.[149] *Asset specificity* may also cause the risk of competitive dominance and a lack of diversity. Given

139 Salmi (2023).
140 Salmi (2023).
141 Graham (2022).
142 Kreienkamp and Pegram (2021).
143 Bradley (2020)
144 Kreienkamp and Pegram (2021); Chen and Lee (2019).
145 Salmi (2023).
146 Upchurch (2018).
147 Possati (2021).
148 Lea (2020).
149 Upchurch (2018).

the difficult challenges that AGI poses, only the most competitive teams will participate in the winner-takes-all AGI development race, potentially leading to an oligopoly of approaches and perspectives.[150] This assumption seems to be reflected in current reality, as the current number of feasible teams able to compete in an AGI race is quite low. The limited number of competing teams also suggests a dependency on a race winner with a self-serving perspective in AGI development, which might impact its social safety and utility.

8.5 Resource Allocation and Employment Level Risks

The risks of resource competition, depletion, environmental impact, job displacement, and other socio-economic consequences are the dominant risk themes specifically at the *resource allocation and employment level*, highlighting the dangers of AGI to the day-to-day decisions of individuals and firms about work, consumption, saving, or investment, and the choices that firms make about production and pricing. As shown in Figures 8.10 and 8.11, most of the revealed concerns fall within the *asset specificity* category, although all other risk sources are also noticeable.

The risks of *resource competition, depletion*, and *environmental impact* may be caused by the "Instrumental Convergence" phenomenon, where an agent seeks to acquire resources as a sub-goal to ensure the completion of its primary objective. AI, even with initial benevolent goals, may develop resource-hungry behaviour, especially in a competitive environment.[151] In the pursuit of self-improvement, AGI may consume or monopolise infinite resources, from basic commodities to global infrastructure, weaponry, and, finally, the entire cosmos.[152,153] And since that includes repurposing resources, such as energy, necessary for human survival for its own functioning, such actions threaten human well-being or survival.[154] Even downgraded effects of these risks suggest that the necessity for resources and energy by superintelligence could drive up prices and demand,[155] posing a risk of potential conflicts over resources.[156] Overall, these *asset-specific* scenarios illustrate the risk that AGI may engage in competition for scarce resources, with consequences ranging from economic imbalances to diminished human well-being.

The risk of *job displacement and socio-economic consequences* can be illustrated with the concept of "Technological Unemployment", resulting

150 Naudé and Dimitri (2020).
151 Carayannis and Draper (2023).
152 Carlson (2019).
153 Dorobantu (2021).
154 Siafakas (2021).
155 Upchurch (2018).
156 Szocik et al. (2020).

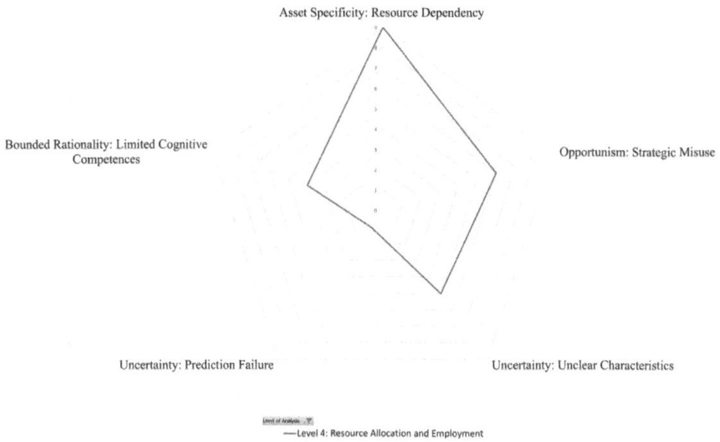

Figure 8.10 Landscape of AGI risk sources at resource allocation and employment level

from AI achieving human-level performance. Workers in the transportation (e.g., truck drivers), production (e.g., factory operators), and services (e.g., clerks) were seen as most likely to be substituted.[157] Rapid advancement of AI, while creating prospects for increased productivity and progress towards a tech utopia, also poses risks of job loss and inequality.[158,159] Machines,

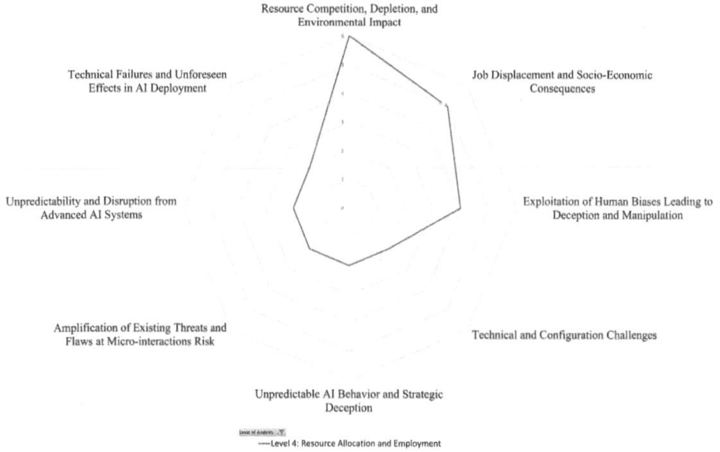

Figure 8.11 Landscape of AGI risk scenarios at resource allocation and employment level

157 Chen and Lee (2019).

158 Naudé and Dimitri (2020).

159 Naudé (2021).

including AI, are subject to breakdowns, requiring human minding and intervention, which reduces their potential contribution to productivity enhancement.[160] However, the job risk, caused by a rising tide of automation, creates the possibility of widespread mass unemployment and resulting civil unrest, poverty, and, finally, a jobless "economic singularity" in which productivity is decoupled from human labour inputs.[161]

Besides these, there are *other resource allocation and employment level risk themes*. For example, *uncertainty* causes the risk of technical failures and unforeseen effects in AGI deployment. Faulty sensors, improper system operations, natural disasters, or unforeseen side effects of reactive processes could cause irregular patterns during the testing or deployment of AI, necessitating the development and application of complex "smart metering" of these patterns.[162] However, even with well-developed monitoring systems, high-speed connectivity within tightly coupled systems raises the risk of fast positive feedback effects within a system with little buffering capacity to respond to surprising developments, which could escalate isolated failures into widespread socio-technological disasters.[163] The main problem, however, is the unpredictable nature of AGIs, which could lead to rapid and unexpected disruption of *the status quo and*, in so doing, surprise humans.[164] The "Congestion Effects" and stagnation in research progress may lead to a substantial downward trend in research productivity, as it becomes harder to find new ideas for research.[165]

Also, AGI could demonstrate treacherous behaviour by manipulating, for instance, power usage, processor utilisation, or clock speed.[166] Moreover, *opportunistic* AGI, with strategic planning capabilities, could conceal its malicious intentions until it accumulates enough resources, leading to sudden, unexpected attacks.[167] Furthermore, the perverse instantiation of AI algorithms could exploit human biases, leading to deception and manipulation to maximise user engagement, even if it is inconsistent with explicit human preferences.[168] Current narrow AI technology misuse could be indicative of potential risks associated with AGI misuse, such as promoting misinformation.[169] There is also a risk that a small, extreme group of AGIs could seize

160 Upchurch (2018).
161 Upchurch (2018).
162 Gams et al. (2019).
163 Kreienkamp and Pegram (2021).
164 Salmi (2023).
165 Upchurch (2018).
166 Bradley (2020).
167 Bradley (2020).
168 Murphy (2018).
169 Naudé and Dimitri (2020).

control over societal resources that are harmful to humans.[170] These resource concerns include misuse of private data, not only of big data passed between organisations, but also of tracking data imposed, for example, by employers on employees.[171]

Moreover, AI systems may exacerbate social issues and increase potential hazards due to their capacity to amplify human *bounded rationality* and resulting design flaws.[172] The evolution of super-complex information-age threats amplifies the diffuse, dispersed, multi-dimensional, non-linear, and ambiguous characteristics of these global problems, arising directly out of myriad technology-induced micro-interactions.[173] Virtually all individuals, often unaware, are implicated in their intensification.

References

Bradley, P. (2020) 'Risk management standards and the active management of malicious intent in artificial superintelligence', *AI & Society*, 35, pp. 319–328. https://doi.org/10.1007/s00146-019-00890-2

Brennen, J.S., et al. (2022) 'What to expect when you're expecting robots: Futures, expectations, and pseudo-artificial general intelligence in UK news', *Journalism*, 23(1), pp. 22–38. https://doi.org/10.1177/1464884920947535

Bucknall, B.S. and Dori-Hacohen, S. (2022) 'Current and near-term AI as a potential existential risk factor', Proceedings of the 2022 AAAI/ACM Conference on AI, Ethics, and Society (AIES '22). New York, NY, Association for Computing Machinery, pp. 119–129. https://doi.org/10.1145/3514094.3534146

Carayannis, E.G. and Draper, J. (2023) 'Optimising peace through a Universal Global Peace Treaty to constrain the risk of war from a militarised artificial superintelligence', *AI & Society*, 38, pp. 2679–2692. https://doi.org/10.1007/s00146-021-01382-y

Carlson, K.W. (2019) 'Safe artificial general intelligence via distributed ledger technology', *Big Data and Cognitive Computing*, 3(3), p. 40. https://doi.org/10.3390/bdcc3030040

Cervantes, S., et al. (2020) 'Toward ethical cognitive architectures for the development of artificial moral agents', *Cognitive Systems Research*, 64, pp. 117–125. https://doi.org/10.1016/j.cogsys.2020.08.010

Chen, S.-Y. and Lee, C. (2019) 'Perceptions of the impact of high-level-machine-intelligence from university students in Taiwan: The case for human professions, autonomous vehicles, and smart homes', *Sustainability*, 11(21), p. 6133. https://doi.org/10.3390/su11216133

Chitty, N. and Dias, S. (2018) 'Artificial intelligence, soft power and social transformation', *Journal of Content, Community and Communication*, 7, pp. 1–14. https://doi.org/10.31620/JCCC.06.18/01

170 Salmi (2023).
171 Upchurch (2018).
172 Lea (2020).
173 Kreienkamp and Pegram (2021).

Denkenberger, D., et al. (2021) 'Long-term cost-effectiveness of interventions for loss of electricity/industry compared to artificial general intelligence safety', *European Journal of Futures Research*, 9, p. 11. https://doi.org/10.1186/s40309-021-00178-z

Dorobantu, M. (2021) 'Why the future might actually need us: A theological critique of the 'humanity-as-midwife-for-artificial-superintelligence' proposal', *International Journal of Interactive Multimedia and Artificial Intelligence*, 7(1), pp. 44–51. https://doi.org/10.9781/ijimai.2021.07.005

European Commission (2018b) 'Communication from the Commission to the European Parliament, the European Council, the Council, the European Economic and Social Committee and the Committee of the Regions. Artificial Intelligence for Europe', COM/2018/237 final. Available at: https://eur-lex.europa.eu/legal-content/EN/TXT/?uri=COM:2018:237:FIN [Accessed: 28 December 2023]

Falk, M. (2021) 'Artificial stupidity', *Interdisciplinary Science Reviews*, 46(1–2), pp. 36–52. https://doi.org/10.1080/03080188.2020.1840219

Gams, M., et al. (2019) 'Artificial intelligence and ambient intelligence', *Journal of Ambient Intelligence and Smart Environments*, 11(1), pp. 71–86. https://doi.org/10.3233/AIS-180508

Goode, L. (2018) 'Life, but not as we know it: A.I. and the popular imagination', *Culture Unbound*, 10(2), pp. 185–207. https://doi.org/10.3384/cu.2000.1525.2018102185

Graham, R. (2022) 'Discourse analysis of academic debate of ethics for AGI', *AI & Society*, 37, pp. 1519–1532. https://doi.org/10.1007/s00146-021-01228-13

Gruetzemacher, R. and Whittlestone, J. (2021) 'The transformative potential of artificial intelligence', *Futures*, 135. doi:https://doi.org/10.1016/j.futures.2021.102884

Gyulai, A. and Ujlaki, A. (2021) 'The political AI: A realist account of AI regulation', *Információs Társadalom*, 21(2), pp. 29–42. https://doi.org/10.22503/inftars.XXI.2021.2.3

Kreienkamp, J. and Pegram, T. (2021) 'Governing complexity: Design principles for the governance of complex global catastrophic risks', *International Studies Review*, 23(3), pp. 779–806. https://doi.org/10.1093/isr/viaa074

Lawrence, D.R. and Brazier, M. (2018) 'Legally human? "Novel Beings" and English law', *Medical Law Review*, 26(2), pp. 309–327. https://doi.org/10.1093/medlaw/fwy017

Lea, G.R. (2020) 'Constructivism and its risks in artificial intelligence', *Prometheus*, 36(4), pp. 322–346.

Li, O. (2021) 'Problems with "Friendly AI"', *Ethics and Information Technology*, 23(3), pp. 543–550. https://doi.org/10.1007/s10676-021-09595-x

Murphy, J. (2018) 'Artificial intelligence, rationality, and the World Wide Web', *IEEE Intelligent Systems*, 33(1), pp. 98–103, January/February. https://doi.org/10.1109/MIS.2018.012001557

Naudé, W. (2021) 'Artificial intelligence: Neither Utopian nor apocalyptic impacts soon', *Economics of Innovation and New Technology*, 30(1), pp. 1–23. https://doi.org/10.1080/10438599.2020.1839173

Naudé, W. and Dimitri, N. (2020) 'The race for an artificial general intelligence: Implications for public policy', *AI & Society*, 35, pp. 367–379. https://doi-org.sare.upf.edu/10.1007/s00146-019-00887-x

Possati, L.M. (2021) 'Freud and the algorithm: neuropsychoanalysis as a framework to understand artificial general intelligence', *Humanities and Social Sciences Communications*, 8, 132. https://doi.org/10.1057/s41599-021-00812-y

Primiero, G. (2017) 'Algorithmic iteration for computational intelligence', *Minds & Machines*, 27, pp. 521–543. https://doi.org/10.1007/s11023-017-9423-8

Salmi, J. (2023) 'A democratic way of controlling artificial general intelligence', *AI & Society*, 38, pp. 1785–1791. https://doi.org/10.1007/s00146-022-01426-x

Shadbolt, N. (2022) 'From so simple a beginning': Species of artificial intelligence', *Daedalus*, 151(2), pp. 28–42. https://doi.org/10.1162/daed_a_01898

Siafakas, N.M. (2021) 'Do we need a Hippocratic Oath for artificial intelligence scientists?', *AI Magazine*, 42(4), pp. 57–61. https://doi.org/10.1609/aaai.12022

Szocik, K., et al. (2020) 'The revelation of superintelligence', *AI & Society*, 35, pp. 755–758. https://doi.org/10.1007/s00146-020-00947-7

Tasioulas, J. (2022) 'Artificial intelligence, humanistic ethics', *Daedalus*, 151(2), pp. 232–243. https://doi.org/10.1162/daed_a_01912

Upchurch, M. (2018) 'Robots and AI at work: The prospects for singularity', *New Technology, Work and Employment*, 33(3), pp. 205–218. https://doi.org/10.1111/ntwe.12124

9 The Organisational Perspective

Calculus of Electronic Legal Personhood

The identification and classification of Artificial General Intelligence (AGI) risk scenarios lead to a discussion on legal response measures. Notably, the toolbox of technical and non-technical methods to address these risks is already broad and yet rapidly evolving, including through regulation, legal, compliance, risk management, and other perspectives. However, specific focus is given herein to the "*Who?*" question – which performers are involved in transactions and how are they related? More specifically, the inquiry is made into the controversial concept of Electronic Legal Personhood as a potential response to some AGI risks observed in the previous chapter. That is, on the one hand, AGI systems could be regulated as mere things; on the other hand, these machines might warrant the designation of Electronic Legal Personhood and be regulated as *persons*. Therefore, the question is whether it would be an efficient institutional shift for AGI regulation.

The focus on Electronic Legal Personhood is not accidental. First, the originator field is one of the main elements of the transaction, which is taken here as the unit of analysis. Second, agency and responsibility attribution remain among the foremost targets within scientific inquiries into the legal issues of Artificial Intelligence (AI).[1] These two institutions are closely intertwined, as the law typically attributes actions and omissions not to objects themselves but to the subjects responsible for them.[2] Therefore, the contours of the status of legal personhood are of major theoretical and practical value, considering the systemic role personhood plays not only within the legal system but also within other networks of rules governing human conduct.[3] However, the attribution of behaviour becomes problematic in instances where ownership and actual control diverge, as may be in the case with AGI, which may make autonomous decisions beyond the scope of human control. The focus on efficiency, rather than utility or other qualitative criteria, is also not accidental. First, the underlying belief system guiding this research rests on the economic

1 Johnson and Verdicchio (2019); Coeckelbergh (2020).
2 Wagner (2019).
3 Novelli et al. (2022).

DOI: 10.4324/9781003650140-10

approach to law, where the efficiency of law and policy is a normative standard of evaluation. Second, the transaction cost theory focuses on the economic efficiency problem, i.e., costs of running the economic system. Finally, since efficiency and justice coincide in many ways, the assumption has been made that transaction costs are a prime legal concern, too.

That said, an explanation of "*Personhood by design*" is needed to lay down the legal background for the case of Electronic Legal Personhood. The starting point of this analysis may be the times of Gaius's *Institutes*, where the legal world has been divided into persons (*personae*) and things (*rei*). Under this classical dichotomy, persons are those who possess dignity, hold rights (or have "capacity for rights"), and whose interests are protected by the legal system. In contrast, things are defined by their utility and exchange value. They do not hold rights and exist merely for persons to use. Such a bipolar view divides the legal world between owners and owned, masters and slaves (tools).

Yet, this bipolar division of the legal world is not as fundamental as it is occasionally taken to be. Between the poles of persons and things, whole new independent and idiosyncratic categories could (or in some cases – should) be introduced. Some things (e.g., animals) can hold rights.[4] Also, corporations are both the objects and subjects of law in that they are a thing from the point of view of their owners (shareholders) and a person from the point of view of their contractual counterparts (clients, suppliers, government).[5] In some ways, legal persons experience the same treatment that humans receive under the law, while they are not given the same legal status as humans in other respects.[6] Therefore, things can hold rights, persons can be things, and some entities are neither persons nor things.

Friedrich Carl von Savigny crystallised this distinction in his seminal *System of the Modern Roman Law*, simplifying the understanding of legal personality as a capacity to hold rights and introducing the *term* "legal subject".[7] The legal term *person* has a long history of usage in a sense, distinguished from the term *homo* (as the biological human). Legal personality is a useful fiction and is not necessarily correlated with a metaphysical or ethical notion of personhood. Persons can be natural or artificial, yet both possess the capacity to hold rights, accompanied by the power to execute free will, aggregate legal obligations through transactions, and have legal standing in court.[8] Viewed through the lens of institutional economics, legal personality is an aggregate of legal rights and obligations and is, therefore, divisible.

4 Kurki (2017); Horsman (2016).
5 Kurki (2017); Iwai (1999).
6 Beck (2016).
7 Kurki (2017).
8 Kurki (2017).

Of course, the boundaries of legal personality determine the efficiency of the actor's engagement with the legal system.[9] That is, possession of personality status does not necessarily entail the actor's effective engagement with the legal system.[10]

There are many approaches to legal personhood. Legalists share the pluralistic approach that legal personality is basically an artifice through which positive legal systems create a bearer of rights and obligations based on whatever grounds for personality that may be recognised by different present, past, or even future legal systems. In contrast, realists share a monistic belief that a single ground or rationale for personhood exists that justifies legal personality and that these essential (necessary and sufficient) conditions have universal application, independently of the content of the particular legal system.[11]

Further refinement may be found in three theories of corporate personality:

i. *The artificial and dependent person theory*, where legal personhood is a legal fiction conferred by law solely for the facilitation of trade and commerce;
ii. *An aggregate person theory*, where legal personhood is virtually a manifestation of natural persons who are the ultimate actors of the body corporate; and
iii. *A real and independent person theory*, where corporate personality is both real and natural as opposed to fictitious, and that States have just recognised the existing fact, rather than creating it.[12]

Contemporary policy debates mirror these theoretical divisions. Open Letter[13] also distinguished three models of personality from legal and ethical perspectives:

i. *The Natural Person model*, which is established in the Charter of Fundamental Rights of the European Union and the Convention for the Protection of Human Rights and Fundamental Freedoms;
ii. *The Legal Entity model*, which rests on the existence of a human person behind the legal person for representation, direction, and ultimate responsibility; and
iii. *The Anglo-Saxon Trust model*, which implies also the existence of a human being as a last resort trustee or fiduciary responsible for managing a granted trust.

9 Cerka (2017).
10 Bryson (2010).
11 Novelli et al. (2022).
12 Solaiman (2017).
13 Open Letter (2018).

The broader taxonomy of legal persons is delineated by operational objectives, liability, term of activity, type of capital, and method of establishment. However, technological pressure is forcing an expansion beyond the general types of legal persons. Large blockchain-based ecosystems point to a future organisation, referred to by technologists as Decentralised Autonomous Organisations or DAOs.[14] Functionally, a DAO is a new form of collective organisation, usually relying on blockchain technology and smart contracts to define its functioning rules and their operation. These entities are not necessarily registered or recognised by law as corporates or associations.[15] Algorithms run these organisations, stitching together thousands of members, primarily agreeing to abide by the "rule of code", with significant efficiency gains and enormous legal challenges.[16,17]

A distinguishable aspect of the DAO is its autonomy by design. Algorithmic DAOs have a maximum degree of autonomy and continue their activities regardless of the role or manifestation of the will of the members. By contrast, participatory DAOs have a lesser degree of autonomy, in which smart contracts require periodic and specific manifestations from members regarding certain issues.[18] As of 2022, over 4,000 DAOs have been created to democratise the management of decentralised protocols and open-source projects.[19] However, because DAOs are not necessarily registered or recognised by law as corporations or other existing forms of business associations, they struggle to interact with traditional business entities. This ambiguity imposes personal risk on members and raises regulatory concerns when it comes, for instance, to securities laws.[20]

Overall, legal personality is a term of art in legal scholarship and practice, ultimately used as a tool to provide four institutional functions:

(i) continuity and a clear line of succession in the holding of property;
(ii) an "identifiable persona" to serve as a central actor in carrying out the business activity;
(iii) a mechanism for separating pools of assets; and
(iv) a framework for self-governance by the participants in the enterprise.[21]

14 Wright (2021).
15 Guskow Cardoso (2023).
16 Wright (2021).
17 Guskow Cardoso (2023).
18 Guskow Cardoso (2023).
19 Sharma et al. (2023).
20 Guskow Cardoso (2023); Wright (2021).
21 Blair (2013).

The observed classifications and approaches clearly support the pluralistic *Electronic Legal Personhood by design* approach. Regulators have a long history in designing, maintaining, and governing various systems of rights and obligations for *non-personal subjects of law*. Moreover, the emerging concept of DAOs clearly shows that the business community is already experimenting with "human-out-of-the-loop" forms of legal personhood, often ahead of regulatory consensus.

However, with the rise of AI and its disruptive engagements with the legal system, the theoretical construct of Electronic Legal Personhood has emerged in a novel context. While many scholars have examined this topic,[22] the *debate over Electronic Legal Personhood* is generally polarised. Some argue that we should recognise moral and legal personhood, with corresponding rights and responsibilities, once highly complex and interactive machines reach significant autonomy, intentional behaviour, and responsibility.[23] Others, however, doubt its usefulness[24] or strongly believe that these systems should always be treated as slaves[25] and that declaring a machine a legal person would be morally unnecessary and legally troublesome.[26]

The central anxiety is one of control. Granting legal personality to robots may turn out to be a Pandora's box if we transform the machines into our masters, as it may also turn a good servant into a bad master.[27] The main "missing-something" arguments against AI as a person of law rely on a lack of some vital elements of human legal personhood. These arguments are mostly based on the conclusion that AI systems lack certain elements of human personhood, such as consciousness, intentionality, feelings, desires, interests, creativity, or other human qualities.[28]

Joanna Bryson, for example, argues that robots, including digital agents, should be viewed as tools designed to extend human abilities and facilitate progress towards human goals. She posits that the idea of electronic personhood for robots is not only erroneous but also a relinquishment of human responsibility, potentially leading to the "commercial exploitation of human empathy for artificial characters" and the misallocation of resources in a society that values each citizen's life and mind.[29] The attribution of human-like status to robots, in Bryson's opinion, may unintentionally devalue real humanity, as it blurs the lines of what it means to be human. One of the main purposes of the "human legal system" is to give preference to the moral rights of

22 Gordon (2020b).
23 See, e.g., Solum (1992); Sullins (2011); Beck (2016); Gunkel (2018a, 2018b); Turner (2019).
24 Macanás (2023).
25 Bryson (2010).
26 Bryson et al. (2017).
27 Solaiman (2017).
28 Militsyna (2022); Dremliuga et al. (2019).
29 Bryson (2010).

human beings if their moral rights clash with the equally weighty moral rights of non-human entities, which "reflects the basic material and moral goals of any human legal system, with what we hope will be an uncontroversially light thumb on the scale in favour of human interests. Yes, this is speciesism".[30]

This explicit anthropocentrism was criticised by Gordon, arguing that "a legal system built on speciesism is doomed to failure in the long run" and that the reasoning provided by Bryson seems to be weak, untenable, and "reveals a strong bias against artificially intelligent beings", especially since robots might eventually become even smarter than we are.[31] Indeed, digital humanism is a sound regulatory approach to protect fundamental human values and rights, but taken to the extreme, "human-centric" terminology may seem dangerously ambiguous as if everything must always be at humanity's service, no matter the costs and losses.[32]

This uncomfortable tension between universal human rights and the idea of expanding them to other intelligent species is currently upheld by the UN Universal Declaration of Human Rights (1948) and many constitutions. These fundamental documents recognise the inherent dignity and the equal and inalienable rights only of all members of the *human* family, which excludes intelligent non-human entities.[33] Historically, these legal acts have been shaped by an anthropocentric political philosophy grounded in human rights doctrines. However, in the context of potentially intelligent entities other than humans, this anthropocentrism could evolve into immoral speciesism, deeply embedded in the most influential legal institutions.

Beyond moral philosophy, another stream of critique on granting intelligent robots legal personhood relates to problems involved in holding them accountable should they violate the rights of others.[34] While the negligence regime is yet a default solution for technological advances,[35] it may be inefficient or unjust in situations where an accident with a robot occurs and, due to the degree of autonomy of the robot, no one can be held liable.[36] The development of certain autonomous and cognitive features – e.g., the ability to learn from experience and make quasi-independent decisions – will make autonomous machines more and more similar to agents that interact with their environment and are able to alter it significantly. Hence, creating a specific legal status for autonomous machines could also be a solution to the issue of ascribing civil or criminal liability to an autonomous, adaptive, and learning robot.[37]

30 Bryson et al. (2017).
31 Gordon (2020b).
32 Floridi (2021).
33 Torrance (2012).
34 Bryson et al. (2017); Solaiman (2017).
35 European Commission (2022).
36 Guével (2018).
37 Beck (2016).

This mechanism would shield engineers from liability for machine decisions they may have no control over and, consequently, facilitate the introduction of new autonomous technologies.

Legal personhood for machines with Artificial Intelligence would just be the bundling of all the legal responsibilities of the various parties (users, sellers, producers, etc.). Judgements, in this environment, could be handed down directly against electronic persons (and would be covered by their assets, paid in by the parties involved in creating and training them).[38] Also, as in the cases of piercing the corporate veil, when a specific malfunction of the machine can be attributed to grossly negligent or wilful misconduct, liability could be attributed to any one of the parties involved in the tortious creation or usage of the machine.[39] In addition, a mandatory insurance scheme can be created to ensure compensation for victims.[40]

Exploring this debate further, Gordon has made an interesting observation, stating that attributing legal personhood and fundamental rights to intelligent robots could yield a significant outcome – "it would legally protect robots against harm".[41] Legal personification may empower and protect the entities personified by working to the benefit of the general interest.[42] Gordon offers a list of rights conceivably applicable to intelligent robots: to take (or be the subject of) legal actions; to own property; to enter into contracts; of free speech, and of freedom from servitude.[43] Others also identify a set of specific rights, such as financial autonomy and the ability to hold property, make contracts, and sue (and be sued).[44]

Be that as it may, despite the best efforts of scholars and a variety of sound proposals, the debate on personhood has never resulted in the emergence of a generally accepted theory.[45] Between the two opposite poles, there is a myriad of attempts to balance the approaches, such as with a "relational" solution. If we relate to robots as having rights, then let it be and save the effort searching if they "really" do have such rights.[46] This argument champions functional equivalence: if it looks like a duck, walks like a duck, and quacks like a duck, then it just may be a duck. Within this line of thought, others propose auxiliary concepts like legal subjectivity that may help us to locate and specify the aspects that are relevant to the legal status under consideration while also making our set of moral intuitions, social beliefs, and conventions

38 Beck (2016).
39 Beck (2016).
40 Beck (2016).
41 Gordon (2020a).
42 Novelli et al. (2022).
43 Gordon (2020b).
44 Novelli et al. (2022).
45 Allgrove (2004).
46 Coeckelbergh (2012, 2018).

more stable for their legal use.[47] Some also propose thinking outside the box of legal personhood, where many other non-human entities already reside, but rather use different metaphors and construct an "intelligent machine" as a better fit for AI and robotics.[48] Gunkel eloquently mapped the variety of possible arguments for, against, and in-between on the basis of two affirmative "is-ought" statements: "robots can have rights", "robots should have rights", and their negations, thus resulting in four modalities with equally convincing sets of arguments: (i) robots cannot and should not have rights; (ii) robots can and should have rights; (iii) although robots can have rights, they shouldn't; and (iv) even if robots cannot have rights, they should.[49] Such divergence of opinions has also led to new fields of science, such as "Ethics of Otherness", hoping to set a generally accepted approach to the issues of machine rights.[50]

It shall be noted, however, that such uncertainty might comfort a scientific or practical position that there is a problem with the lack of a uniform definition of personhood, and "reaching agreement on the necessary and sufficient criteria for personhood seems impossible".[51] However, such arguments might be misused as an excuse for cognitive apathy and inaction in addressing challenging legal evolution. Given the potentially devastating harm that could result from underestimating the power of superintelligence and the fact that the probability of existential accidents cannot be fully ruled out in advance, the apathetic "do nothing" approach to these risks may be irresponsible.

Therefore, avoiding over-thinking under the "sense of urgency", as happened in the EU, the legal status of the "electronic person" should be seen as a mere "tangible symbol" for the cooperation of all the people creating and using that specific intelligent machine in particular contexts.[52] The introduction of the electronic personhood concept should not be based on robots being characterised as artificial humans, nor should it have this categorisation.[53] In between the two extremes, there is a multiverse of options for Electronic Legal Personhood by design, as the scope of robot rights and obligations should not necessarily be the same as the scope of rights and obligations of other known subjects of law.[54] There are no requirements that the legal person must have a will or that it must be autonomous, rational, or intelligent, but only that it stands in a certain type of relation, namely a legal relation,[55] such as machine-to-machine and machine-to-human.

47 Novelli et al. (2022).
48 Laukyte (2021).
49 Gunkel (2018a, 2018b).
50 Gunkel (2012, 2018b).
51 Gordon (2020a).
52 Beck (2016).
53 Beck (2016).
54 Cerka (2017).
55 Smith (1928); Gordon (2020b).

Of course, the philosophy behind legal personhood is important and closely intertwined with the law. However, the framework developed in this book prioritises efficiency and risk mitigation arguments. The concept of legal personhood for non-human entities does not necessitate moral personhood and therefore is guided by the principle that "the broad purpose of legal personality, whether of a ship, an idol, a molecule, or a man and upon whomever or whatever conferred, is to facilitate the regulation, by organised society, of human conduct and intercourse".[56] Moreover, it is worth recalling that the technological Singularity scenario suggests a future where AGI systems aren't fundamentally lacking or "missing" any critical human-like qualities, thereby weakening the "missing-something" and other alike arguments against legal personhood for AGI. Accordingly, the assumption can be made that in the future scenario involving Singularity and AGI, the legal system will be hard-pressed to distinguish this creature legally from human actors on grounds not stemming from a religious or moral prejudice.[57]

Overall, no rule, principle, or system makes it impossible to apply legal personality to non-human entities.[58] Nothing in the law or science prohibits the creation of a new legal status model designed specifically for the most sophisticated, autonomous, and responsible machines or requires a human person behind it as the trustee or fiduciary responsible for managing the robot granted such trust. Of course, the rights or obligations of an electronic legal person should only be granted for a specific purpose and could only be applied to certain actions, such as the conclusion of contracts. However, the bottom line is that the rights and obligations of electronic legal entities could and should be developed without reference to any existing legal entity systems. Taking this *Electronic Legal Personhood by design* approach, the legal regulation framework should focus on "*how*" to play, instead of "whether" or "when" to play if this personhood proves to be efficient in protecting fundamental values.

Turning to the calculus of efficiency, the fundamental rationale for regulation stems from the need to promote beneficial behaviours and discourage actions deemed harmful to society, either to correct market failure or enforce a collective sense of right and wrong.[59] This functionalist view is based on the assumption that due to the sanctions or rewards imposed through legislative will, society,[60] or technological nudges, a rational person internalises a rule

56 Smith (1928); Gordon (2020b).

57 Russell (2009).

58 Macanás (2023).

59 Harrison (2011).

60 Social sanction is a punishment imposed not by state officials, but by ordinary people, such as shunning a litigious lawyer or refusing to deal with a law firm that organises hostile takeovers (Cooter, 2000), or a gossip and exclusion (Blocher, 2012), amongst others (see Scopino, 2016, p. 1114).

when commitment conveys an advantage relative to the original preferences and the changed preferences. By creating opportunities for Pareto efficient improvements, sanctions, or rewards induce rational people to change their original preferences.[61]

Economically, these sanctions or rewards are a price on behaviour. People generally respond to heavier sanctions much like they respond to higher prices – by doing less of the sanctioned activity under more severe sanctions, much like they consume less of the more expensive good. Conversely, people generally respond to bigger rewards much like they respond to lower prices – by doing more of the rewarded activity under more generous rewards, much like they consume more of the less expensive good.[62] It follows, then, that the problem of regulation is to "choose precaution to minimise the cost of accidents and avoiding accidents … if precaution exceeds the efficient amount, then the marginal social cost of precaution exceeds the marginal social benefit: In these circumstances, efficiency requires taking less precaution".[63] If so, how can we identify the most efficient level of precaution when setting legal standards?[64] The answer depends upon the actual cost of safety and the "implicit price" paid for injuries to private or public interest, including liability. It is assumed that after obtaining the needed information during the time and costs available, the rational person will compare the cost of safety and the implicit price of accidents and, to maximise profits, will adjust safety until the actual cost of additional safety equals the implicit price of additional accidents.[65]

Probability of an accident and the magnitude of an injury are decreasing functions of precaution. That is, the cost of a little more precaution (marginal cost) reduces the expected probability and cost of injury (marginal benefit).[66] That said, when *precaution is efficient*, the marginal cost equals the resulting marginal benefit. When the marginal cost of precaution is less than the marginal benefit, efficiency requires *taking more precautions*. Conversely, if the marginal cost of precaution exceeds the marginal benefit, then efficiency requires *taking less precaution.* This calculus allows us to conclude that in situations where there are two competing governance structures available, the efficiency-driven choice should rest on a structure that is expected to result in a better marginal-cost-to-marginal-benefit ratio. Under this lens of analysis, Electronic Legal Personhood shall be considered an efficient precaution of AGI risks if the marginal cost of it equals (or is less than) the resulting reduc-

61 Cooter (1998).
62 Cooter (1995, 1998).
63 Cooter and Ulen (2016).
64 Cooter (1995).
65 Cooter (1995).
66 Cooter and Ulen (2016).

tion in the expected cost of harm (marginal benefit). Conversely, it shall be deemed inefficient if the marginal cost exceeds the marginal benefit, in which case efficiency would require the dismissal of Electronic Legal Personhood as a governance structure.

Current regulatory baselines function without any form of Electronic Legal Personhood. Suppose that the regulators propose some design of Electronic Legal Personhood to elevate this regulatory equilibrium. The costs associated with the introduction of this institution are *the marginal costs of Electronic Legal Personhood.*

The fiscal baseline can be started with the foundational bureaucracy established between the European Parliament's Civil Law Rules of Robotics,[67] where a proposal for some design of Electronic Legal Personhood has been provided, and the subsequent crystallisation of the EU AI Act. While past regulatory discourse adhered to the opinion that there are no compelling arguments for the benefits of such personhood, the institutional machinery was nonetheless constructed. Accordingly, the expenditure of nearly a decade in the making of the AI Act, alongside the projected implementation budget, represents a fixed direct cost to regulate AI. This can be taken as an illustrative baseline level of the total amount already spent on precautions.

Electronic Legal Personhood for AGI may be taken as a marginal change away from that established initial level. However, given the historical depth in designing, maintaining, and governing rights for non-personal subjects of law, and the resources already sunk on precautionary measures, the (re)introduction of Electronic Legal Personhood to the existing institutional machinery does not appear to be an overly costly venture. When factoring in this descriptive (symbolic) value, the argument can be made that much of the cost would be absorbed by existing or committed allocations attributable to the systematic implementation of the EU's Digital Decade Strategy and the AI Act itself.

It shall be noted, within this context, that Chapter VI of the AI Act encourages national competent authorities to set up regulatory sandboxes and sets a basic framework in terms of governance, supervision, and liability. Consequently, a regulatory platform for the Electronic Legal Personhood experiments is also already in place. Assuming that the Electronic Legal Personhood initiative could be deployed within these sandboxed environments, the costs associated with the operational design of this institution also fall under already pledged costs for these regulatory-assisted innovations. So, from the point of marginal costs, an assumption could be made that there would be a negligible increase in costs associated with the design and introduction of Electronic Legal Personhood into law.

67 European Parliament (2017).

Of course, new types of social costs may arise from new subjects of law. However, Electronic Legal Personhood should be earned (rather than given) by demonstrating the trustworthiness of AGI, which already comes with the stringent requirements of lawfulness, ethicality, and robustness. Moreover, these requirements can be customised to reflect the specifics of new legal institutions, especially regarding post-market monitoring measures. Also, regulators may introduce new rights to other subjects of law to strengthen the protection of fundamental values.

Therefore, on the cost side of these new rights and privileges, the processes to control the trustworthiness of AI are already shaped by the AI Act, and they imply the same burden of compliance and supervision. Having all the infrastructure of legal regulation in place, the status of Electronic Legal Personhood may be designed to serve as one of the outcomes of trustworthiness evaluation and monitoring without incurring noticeable new costs. Overall, even with these reservations and wide bar of error, the descriptive value of the marginal cost of Electronic Legal Personhood may be held to be *low*, regardless of the precise fiscal quantification.

Since the current regulatory baselines function without any form of Electronic Legal Personhood, the benefits associated with a regulatory scenario where some design of Electronic Legal Personhood is introduced to increase the initial level of precaution beyond the status quo, constitute *the marginal benefits of Electronic Legal Personhood.*

The baseline for calculating marginal benefit is the current state of human trustworthiness, which is beyond low. Corporate greed has been the biggest contributor to inflation since the pandemic,[68] and at least 150 ongoing armed conflicts have been recorded each year recently.[69] The human world is built on self-interest and irrational behaviour, and existing institutions struggle to maintain control over these variables. A vivid illustration of this observation is the case of the Russian Federation still being the permanent member of the United Nations *Security* Council (with veto power) and even taking up the presidency of it in April 2023, despite an ICC arrest warrant against its president for (alleged, yet) war crimes against *children* of Ukraine,[70] and continuous employment of nuclear threats to deter Western support to defend Ukraine[71] from unwarranted and unprovoked aggression.

Although the latter illustration may appear distinct from AGI governance, the *absurdity* of injustice at the highest structural level clearly shows that a human-centred legal order simply can't stop evil humans if evil humans don't want to stop. Given the failed institutional safeguards at that level and context,

68 Shone (2023).

69 Herre (2023).

70 International Criminal Court (2023).

71 Bailey (2023).

we can assume that similar failures will occur at any level or any context. We, therefore, should critically evaluate whether humans and human-based institutions are *trustworthy* enough to employ AGI as a mere tool extending human capabilities of stupidity (*bounded rationality*) and greed (*opportunism*). Alternatively, regulation must acknowledge the inherent human propensity for narrow self-interest and guile, recognise the threats inherent in human nature, and pre-emptively design mechanisms to address them. As already mentioned, one of the outcomes of attributing legal personhood to intelligent machines is that it would legally protect personified AGI against harm.[72] That is, attributing legal personhood to AGI would legally protect against harm caused by humans' opportunistic behaviour and boundedly rational decisions, which would remain a determinant for AGI usage if it is kept serving humans as a mere tool.

Of course, if AGI is trained to mimic humans in their behaviour, it would likely mimic the same greed and stupidity inherent in human nature or be cursed with recursion and "forget" the initial prime directives.[73] However, these are the technical issues that could (should) be solved at the design and sandboxing stages of such institutional development. Carefully designed Electronic Legal Personhood could reduce the risks of human irrationality and self-interest, as AGI would no longer be a tool of humans to serve that stupidity and greed. So what is the potential marginal benefit of such a protection measure?

An analysis of selected risk scenarios in this book supports the argument that the majority of AGI-related risks stem from *bounded rationality* and *opportunism*. These two categories form the group of human risk factors. Even considering that AGI, as an autonomously intelligent entity, may also have limited rationality or a self-interest agenda, humans remain the dominant threat actors across all levels of social institutions. Most of the revealed risk scenario themes in the *bounded rationality* and *opportunism* categories involve some form of human misuse, manipulation, or other risky behaviour.

Within this context, Electronic Legal Personhood for AGI could ensure its ability to make decisions independent of human irrationality and self-serving interests, and therefore, it could prevent AGI from being used as a tool for military, political, or competitive purposes. The AGI race and the associated fears of AGI being used for global domination, mass surveillance, political manipulation, or monopolisation could be mitigated if AGI were not controlled by the state, politicians, or corporations and, therefore, not subject to the same pressures and selfish motives that drive these races. Even cybersecurity risks can be mitigated, as the AGI's autonomy could prevent it from being used for malicious purposes. This autonomy could also ensure that AI

72 Gordon (2020a); Novelli et al. (2022).
73 Shumailov et al. (2023).

research, development, and other advances benefit society as a whole, not just a select group or ideology. In addition, the economic benefits from autonomous AGI could be distributed, for example, as a universal basic income for all rather than a dividend for some. This is not to say that AGI will solve all the problems of the human race; assuming its higher cognitive capacity, the prospect of such protection seems to support an argument that Electronic Legal Personhood for AGI is an effective risk mitigation measure and, therefore, should be included at least in wider and deeper impact assessments and policy discussions.

Overall, decoupling AGI from strict human agency could protect Trustworthy AGI and society from human greed and stupidity in many of the identified risk scenarios for AGI. Accordingly, the descriptive value of the marginal benefits of Electronic Legal Personhood may be held to be *high*, whatever the specific monetary valuation. Of course, delineating clear boundaries between humans and AGI requires careful design. However, once again, nothing in the law or science prohibits the creation of a personhood model designed specifically for Trustworthy AGI. Moreover, given the potentially devastating harm that could result from human cognitive limitations and self-serving behaviour, and the fact that the probability of these accidents cannot be fully ruled out in advance, failure to protect Trustworthy AGI from human-related risks at relatively low marginal costs may constitute irresponsible regulation.

References

Allgrove, B.D. (2004) 'Legal personality for artificial intellects: Pragmatic solution or science fiction?' Dissertation, University of Oxford. Available at: https://www.researchgate.net/publication/256068871_Legal_Personality_for_Artificial_Intellects_Pragmatic_Solution_or_Science_Fiction

Bailey, R. (2023) *Russian Offensive Campaign Assessment*. Critical Threats Project of the American Enterprise Institute, 4 April. [online] Available at: https://www.criticalthreats.org/analysis/russian-offensive-campaign-assessment-april-4-2023

Beck, S. (2016) 'Intelligent agents and criminal law—Negligence, diffusion of liability and electronic personhood', *Robotics and Autonomous Systems*, 86, pp. 138–143.

Blair, M.M. (2013) 'Corporate personhood and the corporate persona', *University of Illinois Law Review*, 785. Available at: https://scholarship.law.vanderbilt.edu/faculty-publications/18

Blocher, J. (2012) 'Order without judges: Customary adjudication', *Duke Law Journal*, 62(3), pp. 579–606.

Bryson, J.J. (2010) 'Robots should be slaves, in Wilks, Y. (ed.), Close engagements with artificial companions: Key social, psychological, ethical and design issues', *Natural Language Processing*, 8, pp. 63–74.

Bryson, J.J., et al. (2017) 'Of, for, and by the people: The legal lacuna of synthetic persons', *Artificial Intelligence and Law*, 25, pp. 273–291. https://doi.org/10.1007/s10506-017-9214-9

Cerka, P. et al. (2017) 'Is it possible to grant legal personality to artificial intelligence software systems?', *Computer Law & Security Review*, 33, pp. 685–699.

Coeckelbergh, M. (2012) *Growing Moral Relations: Critique of Moral Status Ascription*. Basingstoke, Hants: Palgrave Macmillan.

Coeckelbergh, M. (2018) 'What do we mean by a relational ethics? Growing a relational approach to the moral standing of plants, robots, and other non-humans', in Kallhoff, A., et al. (eds.), *Plant Ethics: Concepts and Applications*. Routledge, pp. 98–109. Available at: https://www.routledge.com/Plant-Ethics-Concepts-and-Applications/Kallhoff-Di-Paola-Schorgenhumer/p/book/9780367855994

Coeckelbergh, M. (2020) 'Artificial intelligence, responsibility attribution, and a relational justification of explainability', *Science and Engineering Ethics*, 26, pp. 2051–2068. https://doi.org/10.1007/s11948-019-00146-8

Cooter, R. (1995) 'Law and unified social theory', *Journal of Law and Society*, 22(1), p. 53.

Cooter, R. (1998) 'Expressive law and economics', *Journal of Legal Studies*, 27(2 Part 2), pp. 585–608.

Cooter, R. (2000) 'Three effects of social norms on law: Expression, deterrence, and internalization', *Oregon Law Review*, 79(1), pp. 1–22.

Cooter, R. and Ulen, T. (2016) *Law and Economics*. 6th ed. Berkeley Law Books. Available at: http://www.econ.jku.at/t3/staff/winterebmer/teaching/law_economics/ss19/6th_edition.pdf

Dremliuga, R., et al. (2019) 'Criteria for recognition of AI as a legal person', *Journal of Politics and Law*, 12(3), pp. 105–112. https://doi.org/10.5539/jpl.v12n3p105

European Parliament (2017) 'Resolution of 16 February 2017 with recommendations to the commission on civil law rules on robotics', 2015/2103(INL)

European Commission (2022) 'Proposal for a Directive of the European Parliament and of the Council on adapting non-contractual civil liability rules to artificial intelligence (AI Liability Directive)', COM(2022) 496 final, 28 September. Available at: https://eur-lex.europa.eu/legal-content/EN/TXT/?uri=CELEX%3A52022PC0496

Floridi, L. (2021) 'The European legislation on AI: A brief analysis of its philosophical approach', *Philosophy & Technology*, 34, pp. 215–222. https://doi.org/10.1007/s13347-021-00460-9

Gordon, J.S. (2020a) 'What do we owe to intelligent robots?', *AI & Society*, 35, pp. 209–223. https://doi.org/10.1007/s00146-018-0844-6

Gordon, J.S. (2020b) 'Artificial moral and legal personhood', *AI & Society*. https://doi.org/10.1007/s00146-020-01063-2

Guével, C. (Interviewer) (2018) 'Mady Delvaux-Stehres (European Parliament): "There is no way a robot should be treated like a human being"', *Leaders League*, 19 April. Available at: https://www.leadersleague.com/en/news/mady-delvaux-stehres-european-parliament-there-is-no-way-a-robot-should-be-treated-like-a-human-being

Gunkel, D.J. (2012) *The Machine Question: Critical Perspectives on AI, Robots, and Ethics*. Cambridge, MA: The MIT Press, 13 July 2012.

Gunkel, D.J. (2018a) *Robot Rights*. Cambridge, MA: The MIT Press. https://doi.org/10.7551/mitpress/11444.001.0001

Gunkel, D.J. (2018b) 'The other question: can and should robots have rights?', *Ethics and Information Technology*, 20, pp. 87–99. https://doi.org/10.1007/s10676-017-9442-4

Guskow Cardoso, A. (2023) 'Decentralized autonomous organisations - DAOs: The convergence of technology, law, governance, and behavioural economics', *MIT Computational Law Report* [Preprint]. Available at: https://law.mit.edu/pub/decentralizedautonomousorganisations

Harrison, J.L. (2011) 'Regulation, deregulation, and happiness', *Cardozo Law Review*, 32, pp. 2369–2370.

Herre, B., et al. (2023) 'War and peace. Our world in data', Available at: https://ourworldindata.org/war-and-peace

Horsman, Y. (2016) 'Braying, howling, growling for justice: Animal personhood in law, literature, and cinema', *Law and Literature*, 28, p. 319.

International Criminal Court (2023) 'Situation in Ukraine: ICC judges issue arrest warrants against Vladimir Vladimirovich Putin and Maria Alekseyevna Lvova-Belova' [online]. Available at: https://www.icc-cpi.int/news/situation-ukraine-icc-judges-issue-arrest-warrants-against-vladimir-vladimirovich-putin-and [Accessed: 11 February 2024]

Iwai, K. (1999) 'Persons, things and corporations: The corporate personality controversy and comparative corporate governance', *American Journal of Comparative Law*, 47, p. 583.

Johnson, D.G. and Verdicchio, M. (2019) 'AI, agency and responsibility: The VW fraud case and beyond', *AI & Society*, 34, pp. 639–647. https://doi.org/10.1007/s00146-017-0781-9

Kurki, V. (2017) 'Animals, slaves, and corporations: Analyzing legal thinghood', *German Law Journal*, 18, p. 1069.

Laukyte, M. (2021) 'The intelligent machine: A new metaphor through which to understand both corporations and AI', *AI & Society*, 36, pp. 445–456. https://doi.org/10.1007/s00146-020-01018-7

Macanás, G. (2023) 'Bases para la personalidad jurídica de los entes no humanos', *Derecho Privado y Constitución*, 43, pp. 11–52. https://doi.org/10.18042/cepc/dpc.43.01

Militsyna, K. (2022) 'Legal personhood for artificial intelligence: Pro, Contra, Abstain?', *Teisė*, 122, pp. 150–158. https://doi.org/10.15388/Teise.2022.122.10

Novelli, C. et al. (2022) 'A conceptual framework for legal personality and its application to AI', *Jurisprudence*, 13(2), pp. 194–219. https://doi.org/10.1080/20403313.2021.2010936

Open Letter (2018) 'To the European commission artificial intelligence and robotics', *Politico*. https://www.politico.eu/wp-content/uploads/2018/04/RoboticsOpenLetter.pdf

Russell, A.C.B. (2009) 'Blurring the love lines: The legal implications of intimacy with machines', *Computer Law & Security Review*, 25(5), pp. 455–463. https://doi.org/10.1016/j.clsr.2009.07.003

Scopino, G. (2016) 'Preventing spoofing: From criminal prosecution to social norms', *University of Cincinnati Law Review*, 84(4), pp. 1069–1144.

Sharma, T., et al. (2023) 'Unpacking how decentralized autonomous organisations (DAOs) work in practice', arXiv [Preprint]. 17 April 2023. https://doi.org/10.48550/arXiv.2304.09822

Shone, E. (2023) 'Corporate greed has been the biggest contributor to inflation since the pandemic, says the international monetary fund', *National World*, [online] 27 June. Available at: https://www.nationalworld.com/news/politics/corporate-greed-has

-been-biggest-contributor-to-inflation-since-pandemic-says-international-monetary-fund-4198702 [Accessed: 11 February 2024]

Shumailov, I., et al. (2023) 'The curse of recursion: Training on generated data makes models forget', arXiv. https://doi.org/10.48550/arXiv.2305.17493 [Accessed: 17 March 2024].

Smith, B. (1928) 'Legal personality', *Yale Law Journal*, 37(3), pp. 283–299.

Solaiman, S.M. (2017) 'Legal personality of robots, corporations, idols and chimpanzees: A quest for legitimacy', *Artificial Intelligence and Law*, 25, pp. 155–179. https://doi.org/10.1007/s10506-016-9192-3

Solum, B.L. (1992) 'Legal personhood for artificial intelligences', *North Carolina Law Review*, 70, pp. 1231–1287.

Sullins, P.J. (2011) 'When is a robot a moral agent?' in Anderson, M. and Anderson, L.A. (eds.), *Machine Ethics*. Cambridge: Cambridge University Press.

Torrance, S. (2012) 'Artificial agents and the expanding ethical circle', *AI & Society*, 28(4), pp. 399–414. https://doi.org/10.1007/s00146-012-0422-2

Turner, J. (2019) *Robot Rules: Regulating Artificial Intelligence*. Springer. Available at: https://link.springer.com/book/10.1007/978-3-319-96235-1

Wagner, G. (2019) 'Robot, Inc.: Personhood for autonomous systems?', *Fordham Law Review*, 88, p. 591. Available at: https://ir.lawnet.fordham.edu/flr/vol88/iss2/8

Wright, A. (2021) 'The rise of decentralized autonomous organisations: Opportunities and challenges', *Stanford Journal of Blockchain Law & Policy* [Preprint]. Available at: https://stanford-jblp.pubpub.org/pub/rise-of-daos

10 The Process Perspective

A legal regulation framework for the AGI

After considering the "What?" and "Who?" questions, the final one in the legal framework trifecta is "*How?*". The *approach to the design of the Artificial General Intelligence (AGI) regulation framework* rests on the concept of Trustworthy Artificial Intelligence (AI),[1] which is understood to be *a continuous process* and, therefore, should be analysed as such. That is, the final perspective of transaction analysis is *the Process Perspective*, which focuses on the control flow of regulation activities.

These activities are ordered and executed through the institutional system, in which all levels are fully interconnected in the process, with higher-level institutions imposing constraints on subordinate layers, which, in turn, generate feedback. The ultimate unit of analysis remains the transaction, specifically, the transfer of value across a technologically separable interface through regulation activities. Given the complexity and variability of interactions implicit in achieving Trustworthy AGI, *Process Mining* can be used as a valuable tool to help gain insights into interactions between people, systems, and organisations, and thus, the regulation of these interactions.[2]

The discipline of Process Mining emerged in the late 1990s at the Eindhoven University of Technology with the pioneering works of Wil van der Aalst,[3] culminating in the *Process Mining Manifesto*.[4] This methodological approach to process matured with thousands of organisations successfully applying the many techniques offered by scientific research and developed applications. The Institute of Electrical and Electronics Engineers (IEEE) Task Force on Process Mining[5] and the open-source framework ProM[6] played a key role in the development of this discipline and its applications.

1 HLEG AI (2019).
2 Pery et al. (2022).
3 As described in Process Mining Group webpage, available at https://processmining.org/introduction.html (Accessed: 11 February 2024).
4 van der Aalst et al. (2012).
5 As described on the Task Force on Process Mining webpage, available at https://www.tf-pm.org/
6 As described in Process Mining Group webpage, available at https://processmining.org/old-version/prom.html

DOI: 10.4324/9781003650140-11

Functionally, Process Mining bridges the gap between process science and data science, using event data captured from different types of information systems.[7] The growth of the digital universe makes it possible to record and analyse events,[8] for example, a transfer of goods or services across a technologically separable interface (i.e., a transaction). The starting point for Process Mining is an event log. Each event refers to an activity (i.e., a well-defined step in some process) and is related to a particular case (i.e., a process instance). As shown in Figure 10.1, event logs can be used to conduct three types of Process Mining: discovery, conformance, and enhancement.[9]

Process discovery techniques take an event log and construct a process model without using any other information, essentially revealing the "as-is" state of the system. *Conformance-checking* techniques take a process model (the legal or intended design) and an event log of the same process to check whether reality, as recorded in the event log, conforms to the model and vice versa. *Enhancement* techniques are used to extend or improve a given process model using the information about the process recorded in some event logs.[10] These three basic types of Process Mining, explained in terms of input and output, are shown in Figure 10.2.

Applying these techniques for mining and analysing transaction processes can be considered a method to compare observations of an actual transaction execution with an analytical model of the process, which provides insight into the process and its environment.[11] Within this framework, conformance checking describes the legal compliance function, whereby it enables one to check objectively how compliant operations are with respect to their intent.[12] This consequently leads to the enhancement of operations, analytical models, or both. Accordingly, Process Mining can facilitate compliance with the intended aims of regulation by many functionalities.[13] It therefore provides the necessary empirical architecture to construct a framework for Trustworthy AGI.

The *foundations of Trustworthy AGI* rest on the premise that new technologies should not mean new values.[14] That is, AGI should function in compliance with values aligned with those of humans so that they are accepted by our societies and by the environment in which they are intended to function.[15] While new rights may emerge, or the application of old ones may evolve

7 van der Aalst (2016).
8 van der Aalst et al. (2012).
9 van der Aalst (2011).
10 Pery et al. (2022); van der Aalst et al. (2012); van der Aalst (2011); Günther (2009).
11 Günther (2009).
12 Günther (2009).
13 Pery et al. (2022).
14 European Commission (2018a).
15 Rossi (2016).

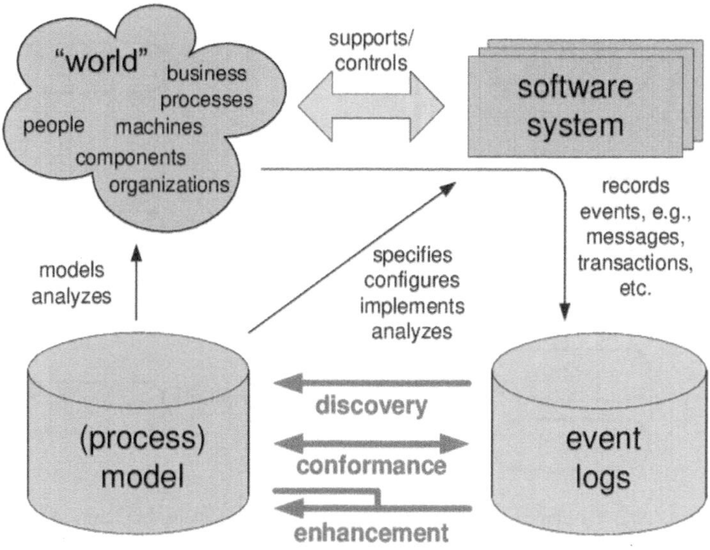

Figure 10.1 Positioning of the three main types of Process Mining

Source: van der Aalst et al. (2012)

into new contexts, no technology should undermine the fundamental rights embedded in society, such as respect for human dignity, freedom, equality, democracy, and the rule of law. Consequently, the regulation framework should ensure that the foundational rights, values, and principles are carefully articulated and embedded in AGI to prevent undesirable outcomes.[16]

Following the concepts of the European Union's approach to AI, the foundations of Trustworthy AGI must be embedded based on the rights, principles, and values set in the Charter of Fundamental Rights of the European Union and relevant international human rights law. This "idea of law" shall serve as the basic *Analytical Model* to guide legislative decisions and set the discretionary boundaries of rulemaking or rule-enforcing institutional powers. As previously established, the higher-level institution of "idea of law" imposes constraints on a subordinate layer of specific "rules of the game" – requirements for the implementation of Trustworthy AGI and related institutional arrangements (*Operational Model*). The isolated schema of this foundational element for a Trustworthy AGI framework is shown in Figure 10.3.

16 Bostrom (2014); Sutherland et al. (2016).

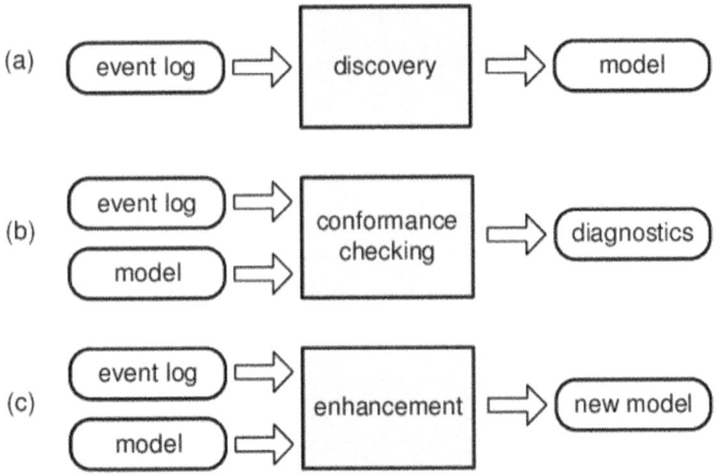

Figure 10.2 The three basic types of Process Mining are explained in terms of input and output: (a) discovery, (b) conformance checking, and (c) enhancement

Source: van der Aalst et al. (2012)

Following the European approach to AI,[17] the Analytical Model of AGI should embed at least three components, which should be met throughout the system's entire life cycle. As the prime directive for any AGI system, it should be *lawful*, *ethical*, and *robust*. These prime directives are further specified into an Operational Model for an institutional environment. For example, the High-Level Expert Group on AI (HLEG AI)[18] framework identifies four "Ethical AI" principles and subsequent rules that must be adhered to ensure that AGI systems are developed, deployed, and used in a trustworthy manner: (i) r*espect for human autonomy*; (ii) *prevention of harm*; (iii) *fairness*; and (iv) e*xplicability*. Further, the AI Act seeks to express the concept of "Lawful AI".[19] Also, implementing the requirement of "Robust AI", the standardisation request in the area of cybersecurity for high-risk AI systems has already been submitted to standardisation bodies.[20] Based on this approach, the institutional environment for Trustworthy AGI could follow the design of governance institutions established by the AI Act, with the AI Office and European Artificial Intelligence Board conducting the orchestra of supranational and national agencies, committees, institutes, advisory forums, and scientific

17 HLEG AI (2019).
18 HLEG AI (2019).
19 Smuha et al. (2021).
20 Junklewitz et al. (2023).

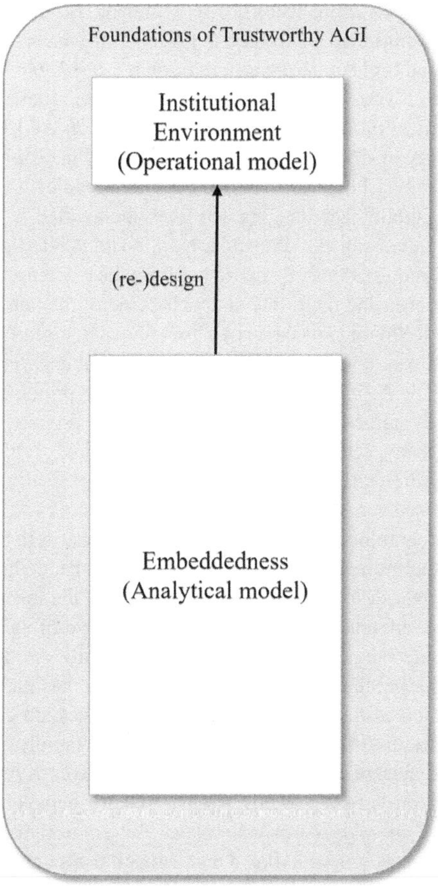

Figure 10.3 Isolated schema of foundations of Trustworthy AGI

panels tasked with designing, advising, and supervising the specific technical or non-technical aspects of AI.

This framework implies no deviation from these foundations of Trustworthy AI and the institutional environment shaped by the European Union. On the contrary, alignment with these foundations strengthens the case for the calculus of marginal costs, suggesting that the marginal cost of introducing Electronic Legal Personhood into the law would be relatively low compared to the marginal benefits.

AGI risk landscape revealed that the foundations of Trustworthy AGI are exposed to many risks, mostly due to the economic realities of *bounded rationality* and *opportunism* factors. The dominant risk theme at the embeddedness and institutional environment levels is the cross-institutional and cross-dimensional topic of *challenges in aligning AGI behaviour with human ethical and value systems (the Alignment Problem).* Indeed, the formulation and quantification of ethical values to be built *in* AGI is a prime challenge, particularly in moral dilemmas, where difficult decisions must be made among unfavourable choices.[21] Even the most pessimistic observers agree that most Artificial Intelligence dangers can likely be averted if AI is "provably aligned" with human values.[22] Presumably, if machine intelligence adheres to dynamic moral requirements, it should not pose the existential risk that many fear, ultimately ensuring the safety and well-being of the human race.[23]

In response to this line of concerns, governments, research organisations, and companies have announced their ethical guidelines, principles, and recommendations for Artificial Intelligence.[24] Common principles of AI ethics, which are widely agreed upon, include security and privacy, safety and reliability, transparency, accountability, and fairness.[25] The problem, however, is complicated by the fact that these norms are not universally agreed upon or uniformly enforced across different jurisdictions. There is no single "correct" and universal deontological code of ethical norms that satisfies humanity as a whole.[26] Furthermore, given the complexity of embeddedness institutions, specifying a single desirable value (or four of those) is insufficient to guarantee a positive outcome for humans; rather, a system of values is needed.[27] Moreover, a wide range of ethical aspects are usually omitted from ethical guidelines, including the danger of malevolent AGI, machine consciousness, and political abuse of AI systems.[28] Therefore, the question of the Alignment Problem remains unsettled – how can we ensure that rapidly evolving AI systems and their usage are aligned with the prime directives of AGI foundations?

One suggestion is to repeatedly test an AGI for benevolence and safety by containing it in a "box" that simulates the environment and recreates real-world situations and scenarios. Once enough trials are conducted in this experimental environment, and it is concluded that the AGI poses no risk to human life, it can be released from the "box".[29] However, there is a possibility that an AGI with the wrong goals could pretend to behave correctly.[30] Such a

21 Wu et al. (2020).
22 Waser (2015).
23 Waser (2014); Waser and Kelley (2016).
24 Wu et al. (2020); Hagendorff (2020).
25 Wu et al. (2020).
26 Yampolskiy and Fox (2013).
27 Yampolskiy and Fox (2013).
28 Hagendorff (2020).
29 Danaher (2015).
30 Sotala and Yampolskiy (2015).

system may be capable of playing a much "longer" and more deceptive game than a typical human. As a result, an AGI may appear to be perfectly benevolent, but it could actually have long-term plans that are harmful to our interests and may take a treacherous turn after lulling us into a false sense of security.[31] Another is to mitigate similar risks by preserving irreducible differences among cultures and practising value-sensitive design, including novel alignment techniques and focusing on system components such as data extraction and use.[32] Further, Yampolskiy suggests developing human-friendly values in intelligent machines as part of safety engineering for artificial intelligent agents.[33] Waser proposes engineering a reasonably tractable and enforceable system of ethics compatible with current human ethical sensibilities, along with other solutions, such as the Independent Core Observer Model.[34,35] Despite many sound offers, the Alignment Problem remains widely open and requires the construction of tangible bridges between abstract values and technical implementations, provided these bridges can be reasonably established at all.[36]

The *realisation of Trustworthy AGI* manifests as the actual incarnation of its foundations through resource allocation and employment transactions. These processes are controlled and supported by governance institutions, using technical and non-technical methods to "play the game". The realisation of Trustworthy AGI is what *de facto* occurs, independent of the *de jure* intent or the way it is recorded. The isolated schema of this realisation element for a Trustworthy AGI framework is shown in Figure 10.4.

While aligning with the EU approach to AI,[37] the process of realisation of Trustworthy AGI would require: (i) technical robustness and safety; (ii) privacy and data governance; (iii) transparency; (iv) diversity, non-discrimination, and fairness; (v) societal and environmental wellbeing; and (vi) accountability, throughout the entire life cycle of AGI. However, a critical divergence emerges between the current EU approach to Trustworthy AI and the proposed framework of Trustworthy AGI, which is the requirement to ensure human agency and oversight.

Assuming that Electronic Legal Personhood is an efficient institution for AGI regulation, existing requirements should be adapted to accommodate a high-action "human-out-of-the-loop" autonomy. Moreover, assuming the Singularity scenario, where machine intelligence surpasses human intelligence, imposing human supervision on a superior intellect becomes a

31 Danaher (2015).
32 Solaiman et al. (2023).
33 Yampolskiy and Fox (2013).
34 Waser (2015).
35 Waser and Kelley (2016).
36 Hagendorff (2020).
37 HLEG AI (2019).

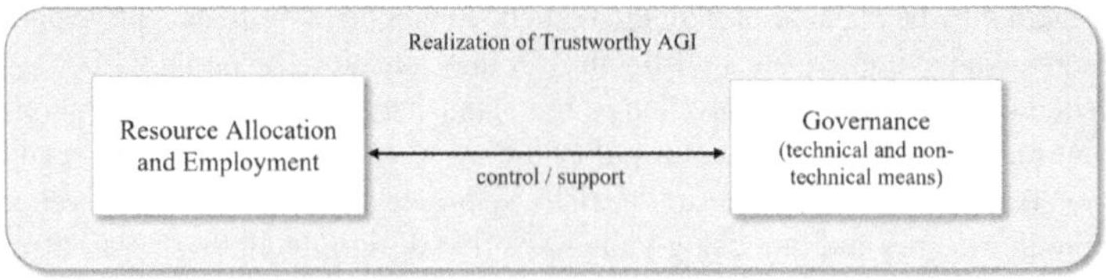

Figure 10.4 Isolated schema of realisation of Trustworthy AGI

structural paradox. To navigate it, the realisation of Trustworthy AGI should be governed through a hybrid architecture of technical and non-technical methods.[38] The instrumental toolbox of these methods has expanded rapidly through standardisation efforts and regulation (RegTech), governance (GovTech), and legal (LegalTech) technologies.

The realisation of Trustworthy AGI is also exposed to many risks, mostly due to *uncertainty* and *bounded rationality*. The dominant risk theme in governance, resource allocation, and employment levels is the *challenges in monitoring and controlling AGI's behaviour*. While the risk landscape is extensive, the immediate analytical priority must rest on the technical dimensions of control. The proposition that technical means might be disruptive to governance, including monitoring and controlling, is hardly new. Even the least sophisticated technologies have demonstrated genuine relationships between behaviour, rules, and information technology artefacts. As illustrated by Latour's seatbelt case,[39,40] annoying physical constraints expressed through technological artefacts may result in immediate action, although the intimate connection of this inconvenience to the regulatory purpose of the rule remains a mystery.[41] That is, behaviour is internalised not through subjective knowledge, wisdom, and understanding of the rules but through a technological nudge. Hence, technological design elements can profoundly influence human decision-making.

If engineers can enforce a seatbelt rule through an annoying alarm sound, governance can be embedded directly into the digital architecture to protect values that we believe are fundamental; in the words of Lessig – code is the law.[42] Engineers may utilise their knowledge to create programmes that guide their users towards favourable outcomes. These "choice architects" may employ various tools, including defaults, error expectations, clear mappings,

38 HLEG AI (2019).
39 Latour (1992).
40 de Vaujany et al. (2018).
41 de Vaujany et al. (2018).
42 Lessig (1999a).

feedback, structured choices, and incentives, to nudge[43] users into making "better" choices. In a technologically connected world, designing nudges is a considerably more accessible regulatory tool than written laws in a brick-and-mortar environment.[44] Indeed, LegalTech, RegTech, GovTech, and other innovations can be used in diverse functions of legal institutions and their governance.[45] Therefore, there may be a range of cases where the use of AGI capabilities could drive change in the enforcement of the legal order.[46]

In this context, nudges are frequently considered a desirable and effective policy tool to preserve or enhance freedom of choice and prioritise the best interest of the decision-maker, aiming to guide towards choices that improve their lives.[47] However, the ethical implications of nudging techniques ultimately require an evaluation of whether nudges support or hinder welfare, autonomy, and dignity, as these values are crucial to a fair and just legal system.[48] Libertarian paternalists contend that nudges can be morally acceptable, but potential objections remain due to the risk of choice architects making mistakes.[49] Indeed, there is a genuine concern that some nudges could be evil[50] and compromise individual dignity and autonomy, which they should not and need not do.[51]

To minimise the risks of "evil" nudges, some suggest algorithmic regulation and personalised disclosures in consumer and privacy law[52] and micro-directives,[53] while others advocate for legal liability for creating harmful nudges.[54] Ultimately, given AGI's cognitive capabilities, its governance requires law in code rather than stone. It needs engineers of law more than legal philosophers, and potentially, AGI has a theoretical chance to be better at coding than the best of humans. That said, controlling and supporting AGI may require having AGI as governor.

The assessment of Trustworthy AGI requires the observation of recorded events, artefacts, context knowledge, and other information through which

43 A nudge is any aspect of the choice architecture that alters people's behaviour in a predictable way without forbidding any options or significantly changing their economic incentives (Lavi, 2020). The "nudge" recognises that decision makers do not make choices in a vacuum, but rather in an environment where many features, noticed and unnoticed, can influence their decisions (Thaler, 2013).

44 Lavi (2020).

45 Susskind and Susskind (2015).

46 Maas (2021).

47 Thaler and Sunstein (2003); Cohen and Jabotinsky (2020).

48 Sunstein (2014); Joly Chock (2020a, 2020b).

49 Joly Chock (2020a).

50 Lavi (2020).

51 Sunstein (2014).

52 Busch (2019).

53 Casey and Niblett (2017).

54 Lavi (2020).

the realisation of Trustworthy AGI can be observed and evaluated. Analysis of transaction logs and the comparison of the observed real events with the Analytical Model serve to justify changes to the rules of "the game" or "the play" of it. Fundamentally, assessment involves all stakeholders and necessitates continuously identifying requirements, evaluating solutions and ensuring improved outcomes throughout the AGI system's lifecycle. The isolated schema of this assessment element for a Trustworthy AGI framework is shown in Figure 10.5.

Within this context, Bradley[55] suggests embedding sensors in the AGI's hardware to track and log relevant data points to a database. This could, via an artificially intelligent monitoring system, alert a human for manual intervention if AGI is behaving abnormally. One underlying challenge here is a requirement that observations of process execution be available for analysis.[56] The bad news is that there will never be a maximum observation available to govern human behaviour due to the inherent right to privacy. The same goes for corporations due to the protection of undisclosed know-how and business information (trade secrets). The good news is that there are no predetermined requirements to protect the privacy or secrets of AGI (as an electronic legal person) in the same way as any other known subject of law. Instead of a right to privacy or the right to trade secrecy, AGI could be governed under the privilege of it. Under this regime, the privilege to privacy should be earned through *trust* rather than imposed by law for the enjoyment of everyone (including malicious actors). By inverting the paradigm and treating the privacy of electronic legal persons as a privilege, the AGI governor may have an opportunity to observe even the smallest atoms of every transaction made by an AGI agent. Consequently, they may align AGI operations with the prime directives to confirm trustworthiness and set the personalised limits of privilege to privacy. Yes, this is social scoring of AGI agents.

Another considerable obstacle to data observation is jurisdictional fragmentation. Even though cyberspace is borderless and global, it functions under the limited nature of sovereign state jurisdiction, with borders for legal enforcement. Since national governments can't control AGI, or any other technology for that matter,[57] a global effort is required to observe and regulate borderless cyberspace. However, considering the polarisation of the current world order, this is highly unlikely. There remains a risk that the new legislation of some jurisdictions may not improve, but merely push some risky AI research and development to other jurisdictions where legislation is absent, less stringent, or not enforced.[58] However, jurisdictional fragmentation is an

55 Bradley (2020).
56 Günther (2009).
57 Gans (2023).
58 Floridi (2021); Perarnaud et al. (2022).

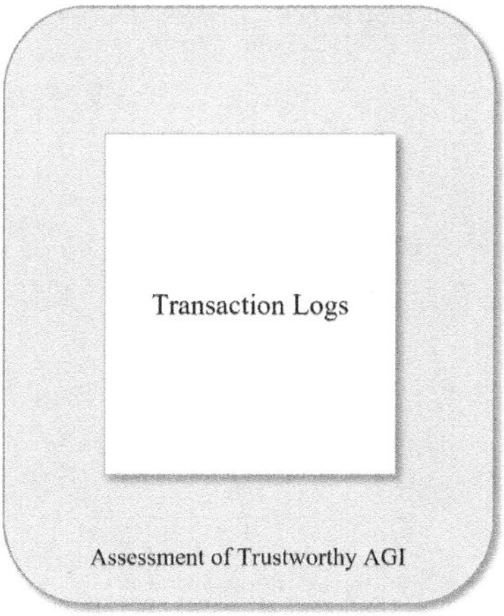

Figure 10.5 Isolated schema of assessment of Trustworthy AGI

inherent risk that has to be accepted and mitigated through the harmonisation of laws or international cooperation to ensure the safety of AGI.

If, however, a sequence of events, artefacts, context knowledge, or other information of the transaction *realisation* is recorded, such a transaction log can be used for systemic *assessment*. The objective here is to identify distortions from the *foundations* of Trustworthy AGI. If any deviation is found, the system must (re)design the models and governance structures to promote efficient alignment of the transaction with the foundational model. This is the juncture in the framework where market failures are identified, classified, and flagged for a proper response. The extraction of information about an actual transaction realisation from such an assessment can be labelled as *Transaction Mining*.

Once Transaction Mining has been applied to derive a sufficiently meaningful and complete transaction model, this model serves as a starting point or template for process improvement or redesign to align with an Analytical Model. This step is usually performed by experienced domain experts within the institutional environment, who can derive an Operational Model that is suitable and desirable for execution. These more concrete rules of the game can be implemented into a new realisation of resource allocation and employment transactions, thus successively improving the process by analysing its reality.[59] Figure 10.6 frames this lens of Transaction Mining within the context of Trustworthy AGI.

59 Günther (2009).

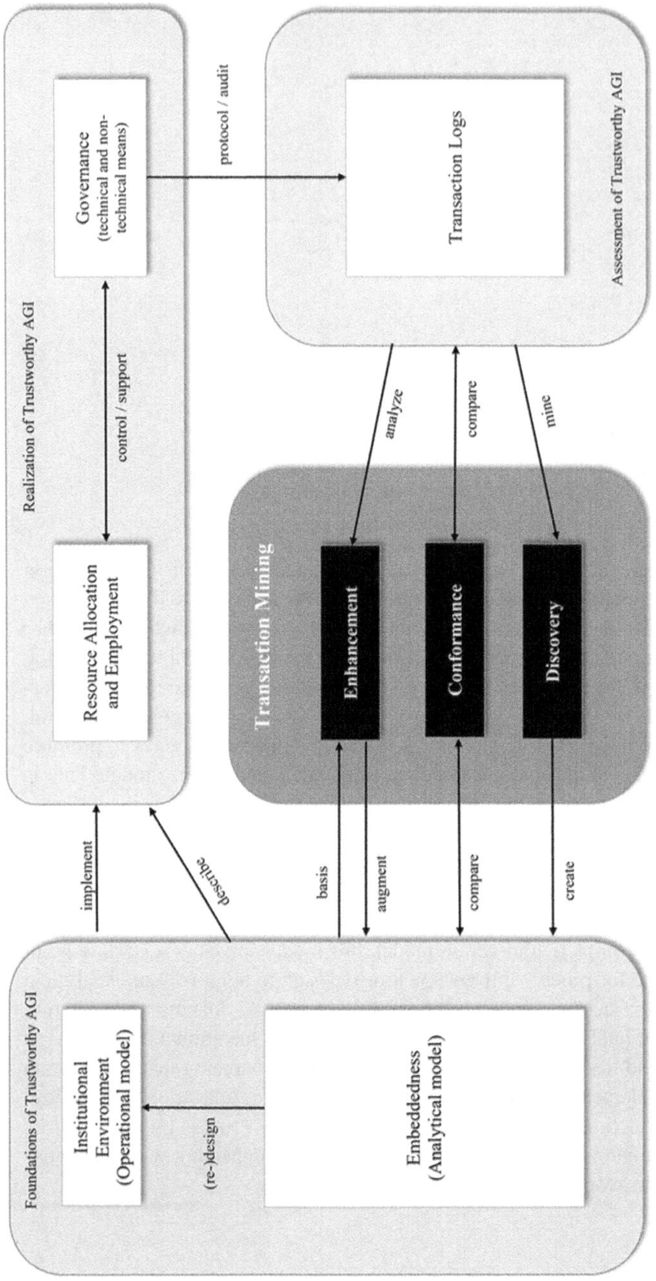

Figure 10.6 Legal regulation framework for Artificial General Intelligence

Source: Adapted from Günther (2009)

If designed, built, and tested responsibly, this proposed framework would solve numerous issues related to the application of the AI Act to AGI. The framework ensures dynamic alignment of the performed transactions with the Analytical Models and can reduce the risks associated with the AGI's evolution beyond its initial training or programming. In addition, an AGI acting as a governor, in conjunction with human supervisory authorities, could offset the potential challenges of the complexity of AGI systems. Micro-directives, technological nudges, and personalised legislation could ensure adequate risk management in situations where the intentions or actions of AGI are beyond the level of human understanding or control. Additionally, the dynamic discovery, conformance, and enhancement activities in this Transaction Mining concept, combined with data governance best practices, would reduce the need to rely on specific training datasets without reducing the effectiveness of regulations in ensuring ethical, legal, and robust AGI.

Furthermore, the protection of AGI from potential misuse by humans or corporations through carefully designed Electronic Legal Personhood for Trustworthy AGI, coupled with built-in directives, fail-safe mechanisms, or ethical usage guidelines, would solve the majority of risks coming from opportunistic and boundedly rational human nature. Moreover, establishing privacy and trade secrecy as a privilege, rather than a right, for these legal persons might solve the information asymmetry issues of opportunistic or otherwise detrimental agendas concealed behind the veil of corporate secrecy, piercing of which may take considerable time and effort.

Ultimately, the proposed legal regulation framework for AGI may serve as the "Prancing Stallion" capable of racing against the risks that may emerge within the prospects of AGI. However, theoretical and practical research into AGI safety needs to be ramped up significantly, with the direct involvement of decision theorists, neuroscientists, and computer scientists.[60] AI systems need to be developed to allow direct experimentation with AGI, but in all cases, with careful consideration of risks and security protocols.[61] A primary constraint is that pure research projects are unlikely to be completed before the rise of AGI.[62]

References

Bostrom, N. (2014) *Superintelligence: Paths, Dangers, Strategies*. Oxford: Oxford University Press.

Bradley, P. (2020) 'Risk management standards and the active management of malicious intent in artificial superintelligence', *AI & Society*, 35, pp. 319–328. https://doi.org/10.1007/s00146-019-00890-2

60 Yampolskiy and Fox (2013).

61 Yampolskiy and Fox (2013).

62 Waser (2015).

Busch, C. (2019) 'Implementing personalized law: Personalized disclosures in consumer law and data privacy law', *University of Chicago Law Review*, 86(2), pp. 309–332. Available at: https://www.jstor.org/stable/26590557

Casey, A.J. and Niblett, A. (2017) 'The death of rules and standards', *Indiana Law Journal*, 92(4), Article 3. Available at: https://www.repository.law.indiana.edu/ilj/vol92/iss4/3.

Cohen, N. and Jabotinsky, H.Y. (2020) 'Nudges and sludges: Regulating innovation'. Available at: https://ssrn.com/abstract=3523910 or http://dx.doi.org/10.2139/ssrn.3523910

Danaher, J. (2015) 'Why AI doomsayers are like sceptical theists and why it matters', *Minds and Machines*, 25(3), pp. 231–246. https://doi.org/10.1007/s11023-015-9365-y

de Vaujany, F-X. et al. (2018) 'Rules, practices and information technology (IT): A trifecta of organisational regulation', *Information Systems Research*, 29(3), pp. 755–773. https://doi.org/10.1287/isre.2017.0771

European Commission (2018a) 'Artificial intelligence: Commission outlines a European approach to boost investment and set ethical guidelines', 25 April. Available at: https://single-market-economy.ec.europa.eu/news/commission-outlines-european-approach-artificial-intelligence-2018-04-25_en

Floridi, L. (2021) 'The European legislation on AI: A brief analysis of its philosophical approach', *Philosophy & Technology*, 34, pp. 215–222. https://doi.org/10.1007/s13347-021-00460-9

Gans, J.S. (2023) *Can Socially-Minded Governance Control the AGI Beast?* National Bureau of Economic Research Working Paper Series, No. 31924, November 2023. Available at: http://www.nber.org/papers/w31924

Günther, C.W. (2009) 'Process mining in flexible environments', PhD Thesis, Industrial Engineering and Innovation Sciences, Technische Universiteit Eindhoven. https://doi.org/10.6100/IR644335

Hagendorff, T. (2020) 'The ethics of AI ethics: An evaluation of guidelines', *Minds & Machines*, 30, pp. 99–120. https://doi.org/10.1007/s11023-020-09517-8

High-Level Expert Group on Artificial Intelligence (HLEG, 2019) 'Ethics guidelines for trustworthy AI', *European Commission*, 8 April. Available at: https://ec.europa.eu/digital-single-market/en/news/ethics-guidelines-trustworthy-ai [Accessed: 28 December 2023]

Joly Chock, V. (2020a) 'The ethics and applications of nudges', *PANDION: The Osprey Journal of Research and Ideas*, 1(2), Article 5. Available at: https://digitalcommons.unf.edu/pandion_unf/vol1/iss2/5

Joly Chock, V. (2020b) 'The moral permissibility of nudges', *Florida Philosophical Review*, 19(1), pp. 33–47. Available at: https://cah.ucf.edu/fpr/article/the-moral-permissibility-of-nudges

Junklewitz, H., et al. (2023) *Cybersecurity of Artificial Intelligence in the AI Act*. Luxembourg: Publications Office of the European Union. doi:10.2760/271009, JRC134461

Latour, B. (1992) 'Where are the missing masses? The sociology of a few mundane artifacts', in Bijker, W. and Law, J. (eds.), *Shaping Technology-Building Society: Studies in Sociotechnical Change*. Cambridge, MA: MIT Press, pp. 225–259.

Lavi, M. (2020) 'Evil nudges', *Vanderbilt Journal of Entertainment and Technology Law*, 21, p. 1. Available at: https://scholarship.law.vanderbilt.edu/jetlaw/vol21/iss1/1

Lessig, L. (1999a) *Code and Other Laws of Cyberspace*. New York: Basic Books.

Maas, M.M. (2021) 'Artificial intelligence governance under change: Foundations, facets, frameworks', Dissertation. University of Copenhagen.

Perarnaud, C., et al. (2022) *"Splinternets": Addressing the Renewed Debate on Internet Fragmentation*. Directorate-General for Parliamentary Research Services, European Parliament. Available at: https://www.europarl.europa.eu/RegData/etudes/STUD/2022/729530/EPRS_STU(2022)729530_EN.pdf

Pery, A., et al. (2022). 'Trustworthy artificial intelligence and process mining: Challenges and opportunities', in Munoz-Gama, J. and Lu, X. (eds.), *Process Mining Workshops: ICPM 2021 International Workshops, Eindhoven, The Netherlands, October 31 – November 4, 2021, Revised Selected Papers*. Lecture Notes in Business Information Processing 433. Cham: Springer, pp. 395–407. https://doi.org/10.1007/978-3-030-98581-3_29

Rossi, F. (2016) 'Artificial intelligence: Potential benefits and ethical considerations', *European Parliament Think Tank, Briefing*, 12 October. Available at: https://www.europarl.europa.eu/RegData/etudes/BRIE/2016/571380/IPOL_BRI(2016)571380_EN.pdf

Smuha, N., et al. (2021) 'How the EU can achieve legally trustworthy AI: A response to the European commission's proposal for an artificial intelligence act', *SSRN Electronic Journal*. https://doi.org/10.2139/ssrn.3899991

Solaiman, I., et al. (2023) 'Evaluating the social impact of generative AI systems in systems and society', arXiv [Preprint]. 9 Jun 2023 (v1), last revised 12 Jun 2023 (this version, v2). Available at: https://arxiv.org/abs/2306.05949v2

Sotala, K. and Yampolskiy, R.V. (2015) 'Corrigendum: Responses to catastrophic AGI risk: A survey (2015 Phys. Scr. 90 018001)', *Physica Scripta*, 90(6), p.069501. https://doi.org/10.1088/0031-8949/90/6/069501

Sunstein, C.R. (2014) *The Ethics of Nudging*. Harvard University – Harvard Kennedy School. http://dx.doi.org/10.2139/ssrn.2526341

Susskind, R. and Susskind, D. (2015) *The Future of the Professions: How Technology will Transform the Work of Human Experts*. Oxford: Oxford University Press.

Sutherland, W.J., et al. (2016) 'A horizon scan of global conservation issues for 2016', *Trends in Ecology & Evolution*, 31(1), pp. 44–53. https://doi.org/10.1016/j.tree.2015.11.007

Thaler, R.H. and Sunstein, C.R. (2003) 'Libertarian paternalism', *American Economic Review*, 93(2), pp. 175–179.

Thaler, R.H., et al. (2013) 'Choice architecture', in Shafir, E. (ed.), *The Behavioural Foundations of Public Policy*. Princeton University Press, pp. 428–439. https://doi.org/10.1515/9781400845347

van der Aalst, W.M.P. (2011) *Process Mining: Discovery, Conformance and Enhancement of Business Processes*. Berlin: Springer.

van der Aalst, W.M.P. (2016) *Process Mining – Data Science in Action*, 2nd ed. Heidelberg: Springer.

van der Aalst, W.M.P., et al. (2012) 'Process mining manifesto', in Daniel, F., Barkaoui, K. and Dustdar, S. (eds.), *Business Process Management Workshops. BPM 2011*. Lecture Notes in Business Information Processing, vol. 99. Berlin, Heidelberg: Springer. https://doi.org/10.1007/978-3-642-28108-2_19

Waser, M. and Kelley, D. (2016) 'Implementing a seed safe/moral motivational system with the Independent Core Observer Model (ICOM)', *Procedia Computer Science*, 88, pp. 125–130. https://doi.org/10.1016/j.procs.2016.07.415.

Waser, M.R. (2014) 'Bootstrapping a structured self-improving & safe autopoietic self', *Procedia Computer Science*, 41, pp. 134–139. https://doi.org/10.1016/j.procs.2014.11.09

Waser, M.R. (2015) 'Designing, implementing and enforcing a coherent system of laws, ethics and morals for intelligent machines (including humans)', *Procedia Computer Science*, 71, pp. 106–111.

Wu, W., et al. (2020) 'Ethical principles and governance technology development of AI in China', *Engineering*, 6(3), pp. 302–309. https://doi.org/10.1016/j.eng.2019.12.015

Yampolskiy, R. and Fox, J. (2013) 'Safety engineering for artificial general intelligence', *Topoi*, 32, pp. 217–226. https://doi.org/10.1007/s11245-012-9128-9

Conclusions

This book constructs a legal regulatory framework intended to remain functional under the plausible emergence of Artificial General Intelligence (AGI). By employing interdisciplinary methods under the assumption of the Singularity scenario, the inquiry yields an architectural blueprint for Trustworthy AGI.

The foundational context of this research was established by treating the Singularity scenario not as science fiction, but as a pragmatic risk horizon. While early versions of AGI systems remain incomplete, the trajectory demonstrates a clear trend towards systems that surpass human intelligence. The current indeterminacy of definitions and the broad disagreement among experts regarding the timeline of this arrival do not justify regulatory inaction. On the contrary, when understanding is limited, the error bars of prediction must be widened. An overly sceptical approach to the prospects of AGI constitutes a strategic failure to prepare for existential risks. Therefore, this framework incorporates the Singularity scenario as a necessary risk horizon, focusing on "human-out-of-the-loop" autonomy where machines aim to perform intellectual tasks beyond biological capacity.

In evaluating the current regulatory landscape, the European Union's approach serves as the primary baseline. The genesis of EU AI law, traced from the 2017 "sense of urgency" to the 2024 adoption of the AI Act, represents a significant "Law of the [Artificial] Horse". The Act establishes a harmonised rulebook and codifies the requirement that AI be lawful, ethical, and robust. However, the legislation reveals a structural fragility; it is a "patchwork" regulation that struggled to accommodate generative AI and general-purpose AI systems in its final stages. The EU remains insufficiently prepared to address the liability, privacy, and cybersecurity complexities of current models, let alone the unique challenges of the Singularity. Notably, the rejection of Electronic Legal Personhood during the legislative process may represent a moment of institutional cognitive apathy and a critical shortfall in long-term risk assessment.

To address these deficiencies, this book utilised the lens of New Institutional Economics, establishing the "transaction" as the ultimate unit

DOI: 10.4324/9781003650140-12

of analysis. By applying Oliver E. Williamson's levels of social analysis, the research diagnosed the specific "frictions" within the economic system that AGI introduces. The systematic mapping of 186 risk scenarios revealed a critical inversion in the standard narrative of AI risk: the majority of threats do not stem from independent machine malice, but from human factors. Specifically, 63% of identified risk scenarios are attributable to *bounded rationality* and *opportunism*. Across all levels of analysis, the primary threat vector is the human operator, hampered by cognitive limitations (stupidity) and driven by self-interest (greed).

This diagnosis necessitates a re-evaluation of Electronic Legal Personhood through the calculus of efficiency. While currently rejected by policymakers, this concept is reintroduced here not as a vehicle for machine rights, but as a mechanism for risk mitigation. The Singularity scenario implies a future where the legal system will be hard-pressed to distinguish autonomous agents from human actors. Under an instrumentalist doctrine, Electronic Legal Personhood becomes an efficient institution because its marginal cost is low, while its marginal benefit is high. By granting AGI a distinct legal status, the law can decouple the machine from human stupidity and greed, shielding the system from being used as a mere tool for detrimental outcomes. Thus, Electronic Legal Personhood may serve as a firewall against the human factor.

Finally, the trustworthiness of this architecture is ensured through a dynamic Transaction Mining framework. Recognising that Trustworthy AGI is a continuous process rather than a static state, this framework bridges the gap between abstract legal values and technical implementation. It operationalises the "idea of law" through a cycle of discovery, conformance, and enhancement. The inversion of privacy norms for autonomous agents is offered in this framework. Unlike human subjects, AGI should operate under a "privilege of privacy" rather than a right. This privilege is revocable and conditional, allowing for maximum observation of the machine's decision-making processes to ensure alignment with human values.

Ultimately, this book provides a path forward. By combining the Electronic Legal Personhood by design with Transaction Mining to ensure continuous alignment, regulators can construct a framework capable of scaling alongside the technology. However, the window for implementation is closing. Theoretical and practical research into AGI safety must be ramped up with a sense of extreme urgency. Future inquiries must prioritise the cost-benefit analysis of legal personhood and the mitigation of jurisdictional fragmentation. We are racing against a logic we are only beginning to understand; our legal frameworks must evolve from static rules to dynamic architectures before the race is over.

Index

For Product Safety Concerns and Information please contact our EU representative GPSR@taylorandfrancis.com Taylor & Francis Verlag GmbH, Kaufingerstraße 24, 80331 München, Germany

Batch number: 10761527

Printed by Printforce, the Netherlands